D1576480

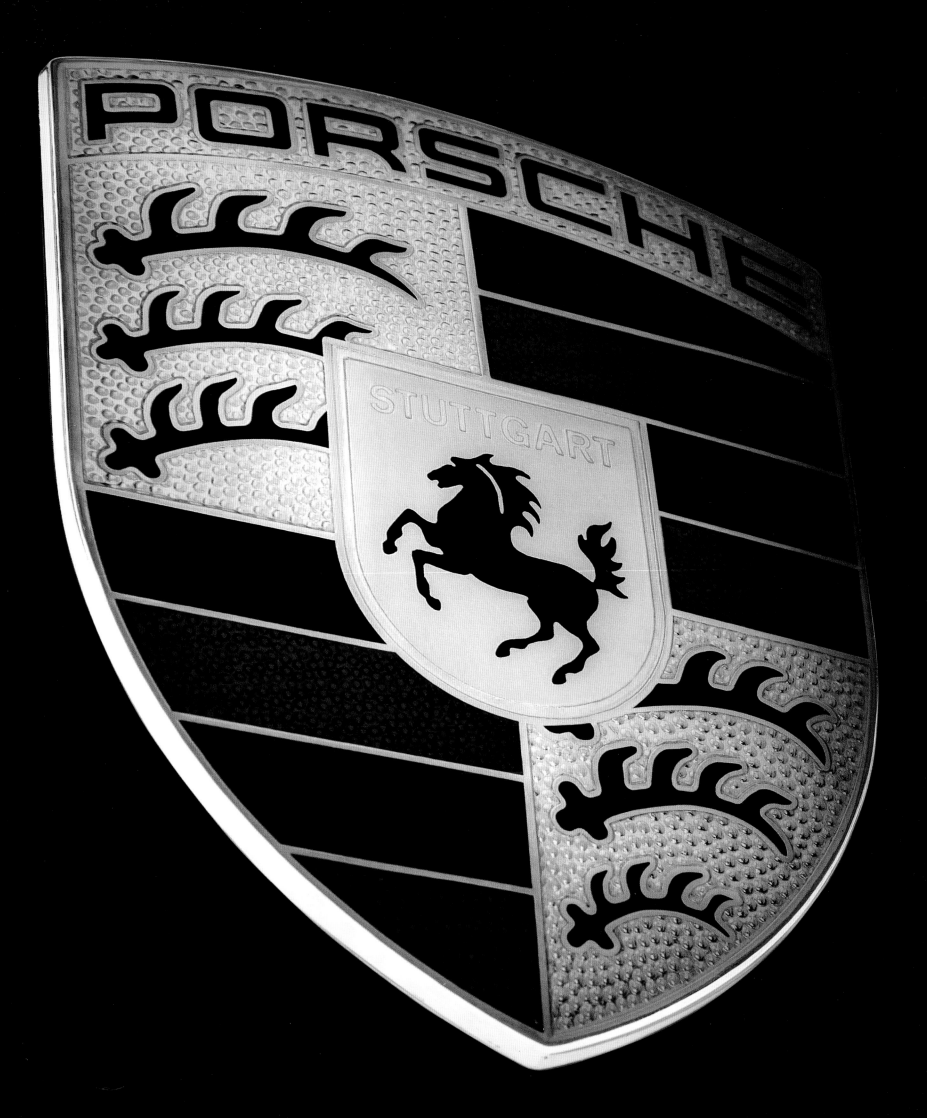

PORSCHE

the story of a German legend

TEXT BY PETER RUCH

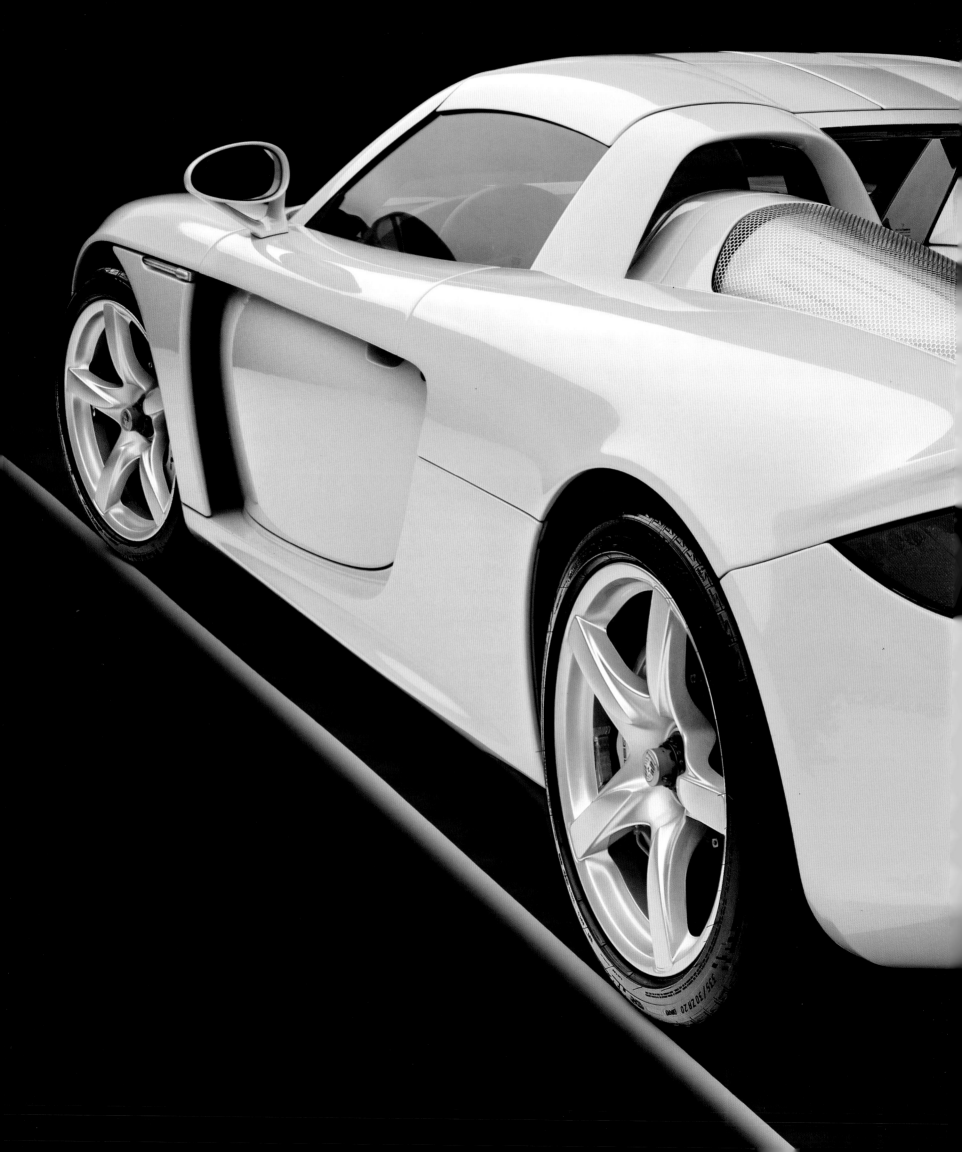

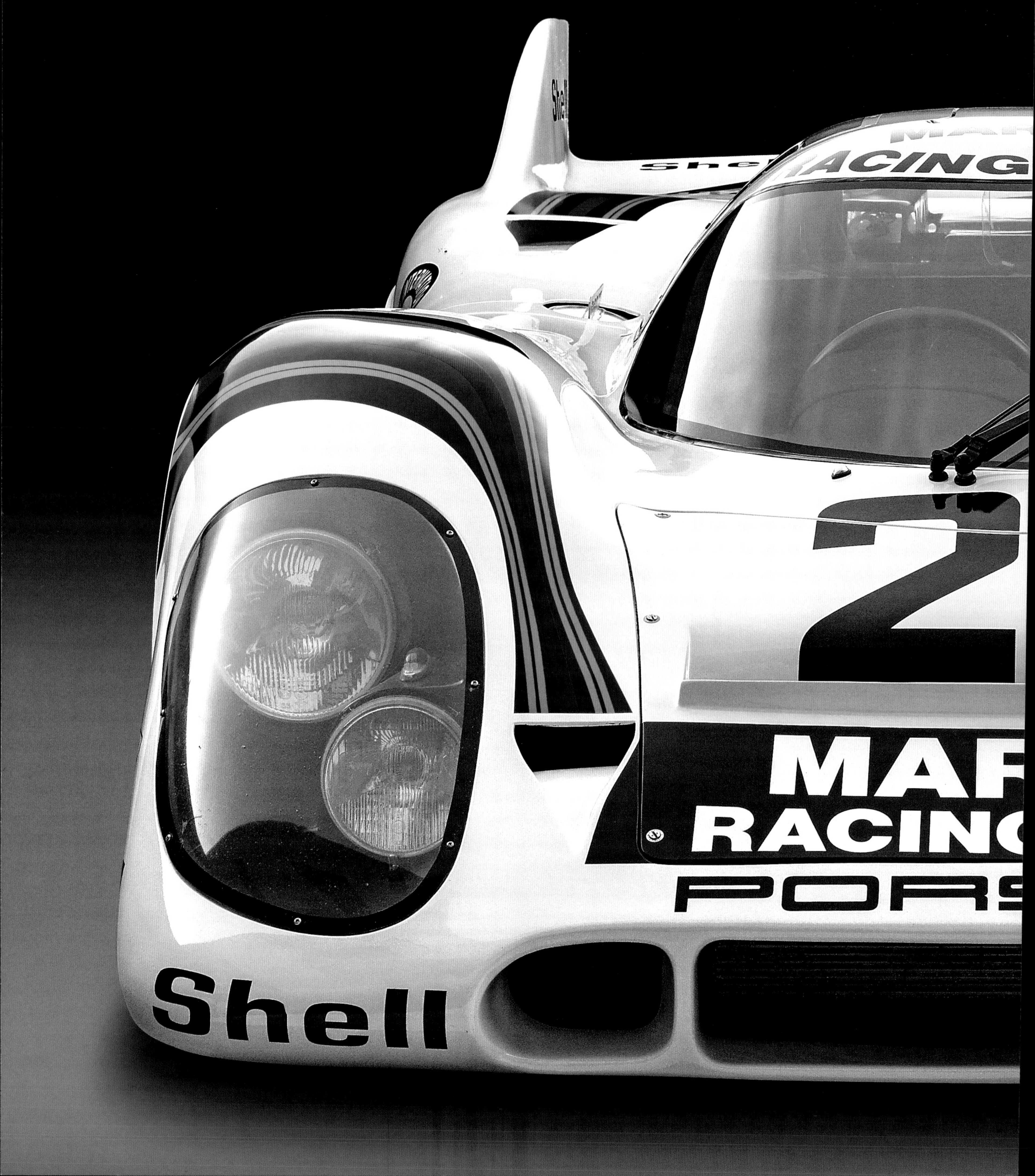
Shell
Shell
2
MAR
RACING
PORS
Shell

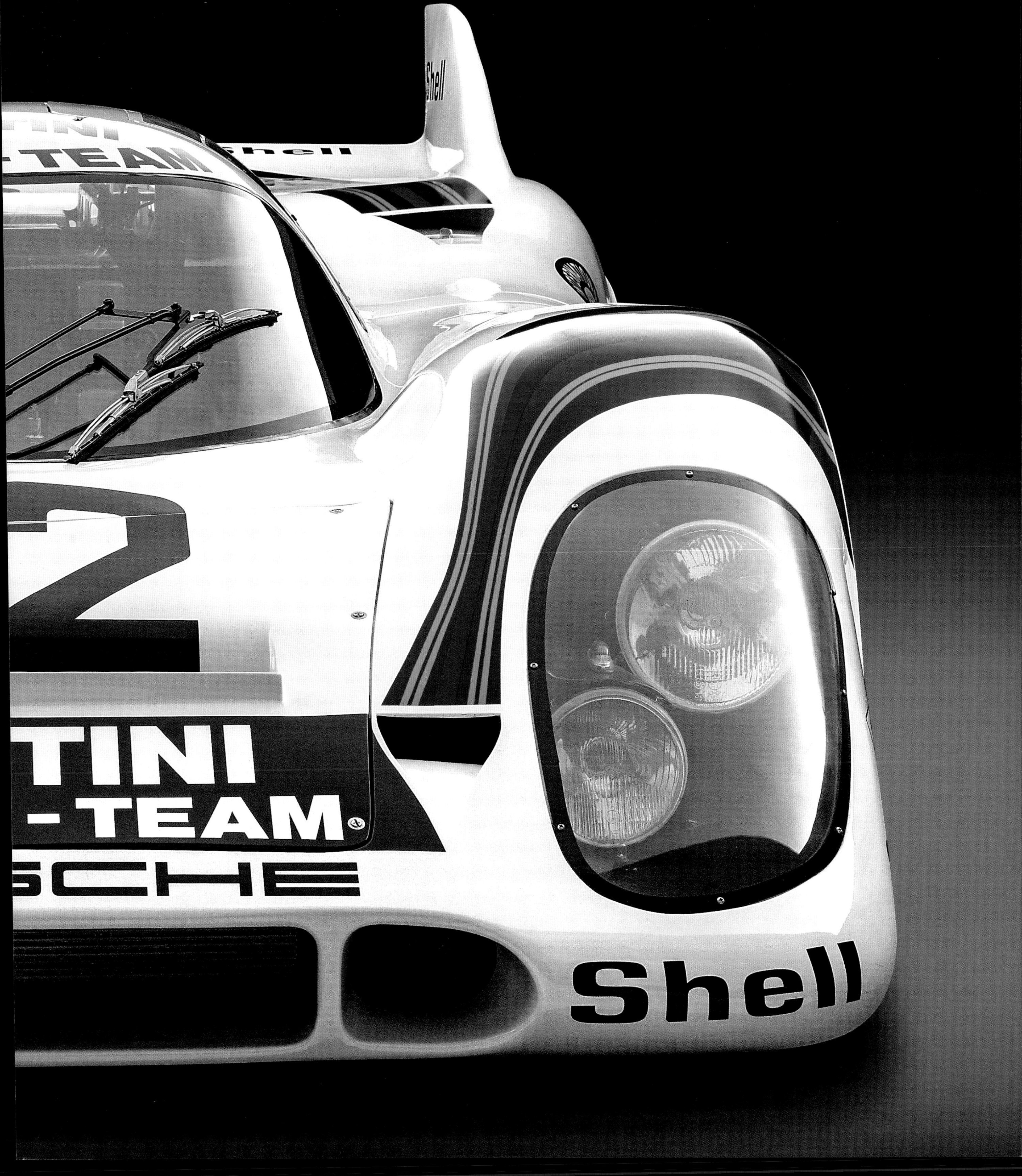
Shell
-TEAM
Shell
2
TINI
-TEAM
SCHE
Shell

Contents

4-5 A Porsche 356 A GS/GT
1957 Carrera Speedster.

6-7 A 2005 Porsche Carrera GT.

8-9 A 1986-1989 Porsche 959.

10-11 The Porsche 917K winner
at Le Mans in 1971.

12-13 Street version of the
1996 993 GT1 racecar.

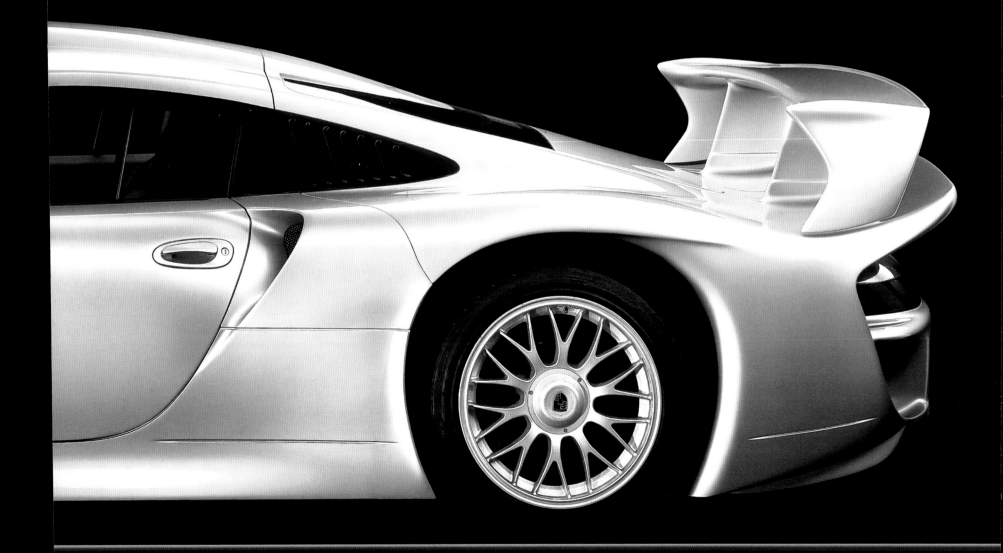

Project editor   *Editorial coordination*   *Editorial assistant*   *Graphic design*

Valeria Manferto De Fabianis   Laura Accomazzo   Giorgia Raineri   Maria Cucchi

14 A 1964 Porsche 911 2.0 Coupé.

There's no such thing as a Porsche myth. Not so much because the whole concept of a myth has become a cliché and because the term is rarely applied correctly any-
more, but because when it comes to the Porsche brand, there's only one thing that has ever mattered: the product.

When Porsche first introduced the 911 to the market, in September 1964, its 130 hp didn't exactly qualify it as a "true sports
car," inasmuch as the models of the other makes, especially the Italian and American ones, were on a completely different level
as far as power was concerned. The image we have of the 911 today is the product of a skillful rereading of history.

Word that the 911 was a "fast car," however, spread like wildfire because, unlike most other vehicles of its era, it could be
characterized as "dependable." And, at that time, this meant it was relatively easy to drive. Most importantly, you could drive
long distances on the German highways at high speeds without having to stop every fifty miles or so to deal with mechanical
problems. Rumor of this dependability spread quickly among the racing crowd as well: and this is how one of the greatest
legends of sports cars was born.

The idea still applies today: Porsches—with the exception of the Carrera GT and the 918 Spyder—may not be the most powerful of the super sports cars, but more than any other car, they embody all that is best of classic German engineering and quality.
Every technical element is of the highest standard because in Stuttgart they're never happy with "second best." Even if, today,
Porsche produces expensive cars (and therefore earns a boatload of money), the fact remains that a Porsche has always been,
and still is, worth every penny spent. It wasn't through a stroke of luck, either, that Porsches came to be worth so much, but
rather it was through years of marvelous perseverance, both technical and emotional. Other cars may be faster, more powerful,
more "bad," but it is the 911 that, for over 50 years, has been the most magnificent symbol of handcrafted workmanship, of
German precision and attention to detail: a true embodiment of the "made in Germany" concept. And this continues to be true
today: I don't believe any other car will let you travel long distances on German highways faster than a Porsche 911 Turbo S.

The story of the Porsche is a fascinating one: this book is dedicated to it. Cars like the ones Porsche is still producing today could
only have come out of a long history like that of the Porsche and Piëch families. The story of the Porsche brand is invariably

15 A 2012 Porsche 911 (991) Carrera 4S Coupé.

bound to Ferdinand Porsche, one of the greatest designers in the early days of
automobile history. He was a pioneer of experiments with electric and hybrid propulsion,
he understood from the outset the importance of competition, and how important it was to design light vehicles,
and he designed what was probably the most important car of all time, the Volkswagen Beetle. Unfortunately, he was only able
to marginally enjoy the birth of Porsche as an Automobile Design House after the Second World War, but it never would have
been possible to build a true Porsche were it not for his everpresent spirit.

With the 356, his son Ferry Porsche who, as an engineer might not have been the genius his father was, but certainly was more
brilliant where business and entrepreneurship were concerned, brought to life all that was quintessential in Ferdinand Porsche's
ideas and preliminary work and later crowned his achievements once and for all with the monumental 911. Even today Porsche
employs more topnotch engineers for a company of its size than any other auto maker, has a highly successful research center
that is ground-breaking compared to others, and truly lives up to the slogan "at the forefront of technology" that other companies like to boast of. The spirit of Ferdinand Porsche's genius continues to reign over the Stuttgart-Zuffenhausen headquarters
where the staff still strives to measure up to his standards.

But Porsche would never have earned the glorious worldwide fame it enjoys today had the Stuttgart team not adopted from
the very beginning an old undoubtedly American sales and marketing strategy: "Win on Sundays, sell on Mondays."

Of course, it all started with the 356 which, by the end of the 1940s, had already established itself as a great option for amateur racers who wanted a vehicle that was relatively affordable. Furthermore, the car offered another advantage: on Fridays a driver could drive it to a racing circuit, race it without penalty points over the course of the weekend, and then drive the same car home as if nothing had happened. Oh yes, and they might have a trophy or two in hand.

The company's fame only increased once it, too, began to participate officially in races with a few of its vehicles, sweeping up its first victories in each of the categories it entered. And it wasn't long before top drivers and famous personalities, such as James Dean and Steve McQueen, among others, were driving Porsches and this further contributed to beefing up the legend. Porsche's first major victory was in the 1956 Targa Florio, when the company hadn't even celebrated its tenth birthday. Granted, Ferrari's car's were faster and had won more races, but their approach was different: Ferrari built vehicles that were always intended for racing and, furthermore, only produced a handful of extremely expensive street cars, while Porsche essentially produced sports cars which it also happened to enter in races. The Targa Florio was a turning point: after that the Stuttgart house focused on the 24 Hours of Le Mans, the world's most important endurance race. In France, this small automaker was able to show off the values it most cherished: superior technology and dependability.

With the Porsche 917, Porsche gave even the racing world an absolute legend, one of the greatest vehicles of all time; it may not have been as long-lasting as the 911, but it was certainly as instrumental to the brand's image. Even the 956 and the 962 were so far superior to the competition, that Porsche had to "reign itself in" because of the absence of competition.

Of the most important races worldwide, the only ones Porsche has never won are the Mille Miglia, the Indianapolis 500, and

the Carrera Panamericana. Considering the company's own expectations, moreover, the two Formula 1 world titles, don't really count. Unfortunately, it will not be Porsche's decision alone whether to try to change this in the future, because even as the superior associate of the Volkswagen Group, they now have to comply with the strategic decisions that are handed down from above. Nevertheless, Porsche is so committed to and puts so much effort into its relationship with private racing clients that it has few equals among other car manufacturers, and has thereby created a level of brand allegiance that is more or less unequalled in the auto industry.

Another noteworthy aspect is that Porsche has always come up with absolutely extraordinary commercials. These have always managed to portray a healthy dosage of confidence in its own image combined with a sense of humor that is out of character for a Swabian company. If you compare it to the competition, Porsche's publicity is a rarity in and of itself. And yet, no other brand needs publicity as much as Porsche does. "Is this a paradox?" asks Anton Hunger, the congenial ex-Head of Press and Public Relations, before going on to explain: "Above all, a product has to be convincing, the sound of the engine has to find its way into the universe of one's heart's emotions and the design must redefine one's sense of aesthetics. It's only after this has been accomplished that advertising can come into the picture." Like we've said before: it's the product, the product, the product. Everything else is just the cherry on top.

In the 1970s, when I was a child, my father took me to see several races; I sat on his shoulders. At that time, I was especially fascinated by the shape of the Porsches and by the sound of their engines. A few years later, when I wrote to some of my favorite auto makers begging them to send me catalogs and posters, I received from Porsche everything that the heart of a little boy could possibly wish for. They did this despite the fact that in those days, Porsche's financial standing was all but rosy. And so it was in those years that the foundations were laid for a relationship of boundless love, the kind of love that isn't grounded in reason, but that is filial, and it continues to today. Yes, I too belong to that hardcore group for whom any product other than the 911 isn't really a "true Porsche" since the "outsiders," like the Cayenne and the new Macan, will never fully make their way into my soul. Nevertheless, I do have to hand it to them for bringing so much financial success to the Stuttgart company, especially as, when all is said and done, this has also been beneficial to the beloved 911.

Today Porsche is part of a large and powerful group, belonging to Volkswagen Group. One could let oneself be unhappy about this, but one shouldn't necessarily do so. Yes, one might take exception to some of the joint venture strategies, but after all, all the major auto producers are operating like this now; one could also be happy about the fact that this translates to reduced production costs which, in turn, means more opportunities for innovation.

Not everything coming out of Stuttgart is quite as grandiose as the 911 but, for example, when you sit at the wheel of a Panamera, when you drive it (preferably on a long journey through the night), you'll find it is actually an extraordinary car. And the Boxster: there's absolutely nothing the matter with it, even though it'll never shed its image of being "the beauty salon owner's Porsche." And the Cayman? It comes perilously close to the 911 and, consequently, has had the brakes put on it by Porsche itself. As far as the Cayenne and the Macan are concerned, I plead the 5th in my capacity as a sports car fanatic (even though I've expressed my opinion on the subject more than enough...). For all intents and purposes, over the course of the last 20 years,

Porsche has distanced itself from its core group of clients especially in terms of pricing, but you can't really blame the Stuttgart team for this, because they continue to develop extraordinary products, and there's always someone who is willing to spend what it takes to own one. Truth be told, the exclusivity element just can't be ignored, otherwise we'd risk finding a Porsche on every corner. At any rate, those who can't fork over the cash for the latest model can always be just as happy with a used model because there's no other brand with such a high percentage of previously owned cars still on the road. Once again, it all goes back to that dependability. Over the course of the last 30 years I've had the pleasure of driving just about every new Porsche introduced to the market. Some of the older models, like the first 911 and the first 356, along with this and that racing car, have even had the distinction of becoming part of my "auto park." The fascination with the 911 continues, uninterrupted. You put the key in on the left, turn it gently to the right, and the flat six comes to life with that slight rumble, that unmistakable growl: the ritual has been the same for the past 50 years. This mellifluous backdrop has remained more or less the same today, even if now the engines are water-cooled, instead of air-cooled, and the power output isn't on the order of 130 hp, but up to 560. For over 50 years, the attraction hasn't wavered because, subconsciously, we know that the pleasure we will experience will be substantial. Just as we know that we may want to make the drive to the office a little longer than usual. In the past there was a famous ad slogan that went: "You can spend more time on your breakfast and still get home earlier." A classic commercial, indeed, but not necessarily accurate. The Porsche driver, in fact, doesn't always drive around with the pedal to the metal, because he knows what his car is capable of and just knowing it is enough, at least if he has any feelings at all for his car.

20-21 A 1967 Porsche 911.

A Night in the Museum

Three years in the making, the futuristic architecture of the new Porsche Museum was inaugurated at Zuffenhausen's Porscheplatz in early 2009. This new symbol of the city of Stuttgart sits close to the site of the historic Porsche headquarters and is supported by three V-shaped columns of reinforced concrete that give the main structure the appearance of floating in space. Within the exhibition area, eighty different vehicles are shown on a continuously rotating basis.

Collaborating with the architectural firm of Dugan Meissel, Porsche has created a space that, up to just a few years ago, would not have been technically feasible. Knowledge of building materials and the engineering skills needed to use them were simply not sufficiently advanced to make possible the construction of such a bold architectural monolith to house the exhibition space that seems to be suspended in pure air and that, at 38,500 short tons (35,000 metric tons), weighs as much as the Eiffel Tower in Paris.

The color scheme of the interior is primarily black and white. Any splashes of color one sees are part of the exhibited vehicles themselves. The layout of the exhibition space, which was designed by HG Merz, reflects Porsche's confident vision of its brand. This brand requires no artificial amusement park-like space for its showcase. It lets the cars speak for themselves. Visitors to the Porsche Museum will find that it is barrier-free and that it subscribes to the concept of a 'rolling museum'. Almost all the vehicles on display are road-ready and can be easily transferred to the street, via an elevator, ready to participate in races or car shows.

Not unlike the floating monolith, with its three-pronged columnar support system, the contents of the museum are also presented on the basis of three supporting themes. Central among these is the history of Porsche AG and its products. This is presented in chronological order along the walls of the exhibit space. At the beginning of the time line is the mother of all Porsches, the legendary Type 64. The line then splits off into two directions. Along one, we see the history of the Porsche up to 1948 and along the other, the history of the Porsche after 1948, the

22-23 The monumental Porsche Museum, that seems to float in space, dominates Zuffenhausen's Porscheplatz in Stuttgart. The architectural design is the work of the Austrian firm Dugan Meissel.

year when the Type 356 was first introduced. Against this backdrop, Porsche Museum visitors can see just about every production model ever made, including the most important racecars. Also on display are all the technically innovative components that have played a significant role in the evolution of the Porsche.

In addition to the exhibition space, the museum also houses the Porsche Archives, and a workshop that is exclusively dedicated to the restoration of classic vehicles. This workshop is fully visible to the museum visitor through a glass partition. Its team of Porsche crafts people and mechanics is available not only to restore and maintain the museum's fleet of vehicles, or Porsche's own collection, but also those of private customers.

This author had the unique privilege of spending an entire night, alone, inside the museum. What follows is an account of this most unusual experience.

Sometimes our actions may appear odd to others, but when one has a particularly intense relationship with cars, some allowances should be made. Still, we're surprised when someone lets us get away with something just because of this intense relation- ship. I guess we're amazed to find there are other people out there, other car fanatics, who understand this and are therefore willing to make allowances for our obsessions.

When I first tried to explain to the manager of the Porsche Museum press office that I'd really like to spend some intimate time with certain Porsche models I ran up against a few obstacles. "What is it, exactly, that you think you are going to do?" she asked me with some concern. "It's really very simple," I said "All I want to do is bring a sleeping bag and sleep beside a car." "And why on earth would you want to do such a thing?" she insisted.

24-25 What is amazing about this building is its sheer size. Even when the number of visitors to the museum is at its highest, there is a sense that there is plenty of space.

25 Visitors enter the main museum via an escalator that leads up from the main lobby. This provides a moment of quiet before the hustle and bustle of the exhibition.

I have to admit that she did have a point - why *did* I want to spend a night in the Porsche Museum in Stuttgart? To tell the truth I didn't have a good answer. No, that's not true. Actually, I did have an answer, but it wasn't one that she would have liked and it wasn't likely going to convince her to give me the permission I needed to spend the night there. So I started to blab something about the profoundly intellectual experience of scrutinizing the museum's architecture and exhibited works and about the sensitive nature of exploring the museum's space, describing it as something that could be fully appreciated only in the peace and tranquility of absolute solitude. The lady was still skeptical, but she did grant me permission. I know she didn't really understand, because it was late into the night before she actually left me alone with my photographer.

So, what does a Porsche fanatic do when he has at his disposal an entire museum, a sumptuous 62,000 square foot (5,600 square meters) building, let alone one designed by the Austriaokn firm Delugan Meissl Associated Architects, and inaugurated on January 31st, 2009 at a cost of 138 million dollars (100 million euro)? Easy. He admires everything in peace. The feeling you get when you're visiting a museum on your own, and you haven't got other visitors noisily milling about you, is completely different. All it takes is two hours to take a full tour of the museum. Even if you take the time to read all the exhibit information. Time enough to be in awe of or get excited about some particular vehicle, like the 1987 H50 prototype, or the four-door version of the 928. Why, I wonder, did they never produce this one? Fortunately, the 1994 C88, another project aimed at the Chinese market, never made its way onto our roads, neither did the Type 915, a 1970 version of the 911 that was 35 cm longer, and that was meant to transform the greatest sports car of the last 40 years into a four-seater.

After two hours spent in this manner, the fan of classic cars starts to do things that seem purely crazy to "normal" people. I stretch out beneath the vehicles to admire the structure of their exhaust systems. What do I learn? On the old Porsches they are run of the mill stuff. In fact, even the standard equipment doesn't do much for me, though on the more recent models exhausts start to become interesting. The true treats are on the vehicles built for competition, particularly those from the 50s and 60s. The 1954 550 Spyder, for example, is a beauty. The four-cylinder engine has only a 1.5-liter capacity, but the exhaust system is huge. Better still is the 1960 718 RS 60 Spyder. This too is a four-cylinder, but it has a 1.6-liter capacity and at 160, its horsepower output is nothing to laugh at. This one boasts Targa Florio and 12 Hours of Sebring victories. It earned Porsche its first big wins in the US.

My favorite one, however, is a different one. It's a 718, as well, but the eight-cylinder, 2.0-liter capacity 1962 version of the W-RS Spyder. Its exhaust system is a true work of art. It reminds me of a Jean Tinguely or, even more, of a Henry Moore.

It must have been the way in which I was able to lie beneath the little "grandmother" — that's the loving nickname the 718 W-RS was given after its long (1961 to 1964) competition history — to sneak a peek at its private parts.

26-27 The entire history of Porsche is on display here, with the first 356 center stage front and, not far behind, the legendary racecar nicknamed "Sascha."

28-29 The Porsche Museum always has new attractions to offer, thanks to continuously rotating special exhibitions. Top left, a Porsche tractor.

SCHNELL

PORSCHE

K 45 · 286

PORSCHE 356 AMERICA ROADSTER

There are a few other aged Porsches I can admire in peace now, too. I've brought along a few history books since I now have the luxury of being able to look at what I am reading about. I start with the 550, the 1954 model, to be precise, which was the first Porsche designed specifically for competition. I open one of my books and read a chapter about the Mille Miglia in which Hans Herrmann drove this very vehicle beneath a railroad crossing gate that was coming down, or had just come down (the literature on this subject is inconsistent); pilot and vehicle both made it below the gate, unscathed.

Then there is this other 1956 550 A Spyder. That's right, it's James Dean's car, the one he was driving to an auto rally when another driver crossed the center line and crashed into him. I like the 1960 356 B 1600 GS Carrera GTL Abarth, too, and the 1963 356 B 2000 GS Carrera GT, nicknamed "three-pointed scraper" for its unusual shape. This was the last Porsche to have an aluminum body.

Then I move on to the 904 Carrera GTS, designed by Ferdinand Alexander Porsche. In 1964 this was the first Porsche to sport a body made of plastic materials. It was one of the most beautiful race cars of its time, as was its "big sister" the 1966 906 Carrera 6, Porsche's first true racing thoroughbred with a 2.0-liter capacity, 210 hp, and a top speed of 280 km/h. This car won the 50th Targa Florio.

I could go on and on but it's time to go to sleep. It's after midnight and I'm done with my close-up look at the exhaust systems and my history lessons. So I start to wander about to look for the best place to lie down to go to sleep. First I try out a spot beneath the 1987 962 C, the one in which Stuck/Bell/Holbert won Le Mans. When I say "beneath," I mean it literally because the 962 is hanging from the ceiling in the Porsche Museum. It was exhibited this way to highlight the level of downforce this vehicle generated.

After a bit, I start to get nervous, even though I am convinced that Porsche is as meticulous in planning its exhibits as it is in designing its cars. But, when all is said and done there is no need for me to be shred to pieces in my sleep by a car that won at Le Mans. I'm not exactly comfortable in the company of the older models either: besides, lying down beside the fabulous 1973 Carrera RS 2.7 would seem too predictable, wouldn't it? Admittedly, it is truly stupendous. Who knows why Porsche doesn't make more cars like this one? Small, light, noisy and fast.

30-31 Formula 1 in its infancy. The 1962 804 model is one of the museum's most valuable exhibits. This single-seater won the French Grand Prix in 1962.

Now I can admit it. I knew from the start which car I wanted to sleep beside. My favorite Porsches have always been the 917s which, starting in 1969, annihilated every other type of competition on the race track to then go on and win Porsche's first overall victory at Le Mans in 1970. Its most powerful version, the 1973 917/30, produced maximum power of 1,200 hp.

All the extraordinary cars and winners of the 1970 and 1971 Le Mans are on exhibit at the museum. The most beautiful of these is the 1970 car, the one with red and white paint and the competition number 23. Hans Herrmann and Richard Attwood knocked out the competition under a torrential rain.

Then I catch my first glimpse of 'her'. It was inevitable. We were bound to meet sooner or later. I knew she was here. I just had to find her: the love of my life. And there she finally was, right in front of me, so peaceful and so uniquely beautiful. Small nose, long legs, such feminine/curvaceous hips. Incomparable. True, her face is a touch too rosy, but when she looks at me with those four eyes I lose myself in her completely. Nicknamed "Der Truffeljäger" (the truffle hunter, in German), but also known as the "pink pig," this 1971 model, officially known as the 917/20, was Porsche's effort at combining the advantages of the long and short-tailed coupes. The idea behind its unusual color scheme, based on drawings of the cuts of meat from a pig, with the names of the cuts written on the car, was probably Anatole Lapine's. Eventually he would become the head of design at Porsche.

So, there I was stretched out beneath the car, cross-wise, so that I could best admire the 4.9-liter, twelve cylinder engine with its approximately 600 hp, enough power to propel the pink pig to 360 km/h on the Le Mans straight. Also nicknamed "Dicke Berta" ("Fat Bertha"), the 917/20 is one of the few 917 to have never picked up a major win; maybe it's this that makes this "pig" even more lovable. A vehicle like this one, even if it's in a museum, gives off a certain odor. Of course, the tank is empty, but your nose will still smell the gasoline. You can smell the oil too and, stronger still, you'll smell the rubber. Maybe because I had my ear practically glued to the "pig's" right rear tire, just to get close to her. I'm not sure, but I might have even tried to hug her while I was sleeping.

32 Some of the permanent exhibit vehicles are veterans of the Targa Florio, the scene of some of Porsche's greatest racecar victories.

33 The museum's collection of 917s is absolutely unique. This is the only place where one can follow the step-by-step evolution of this model.

34-35 The vehicle that played the leading role in the 1939 Berlin-Rome race might well considered the forerunner of all vehicles bearing the Porsche name. For this reason, it is exhibited in a highly visible part of the museum.

Ferdinand Porsche

36 *The Austro-Daimler "Sascha," designed by Ferdinand Porsche, won the 1.1-liter category in the 1922 Targa Florio.*

37 top *Ferdinand Porsche at the wheel of the Lohner-Porsche, also known as the P1 or "Semper Vivus" (Always Alive). The vehicle is still in existence today.*

Ferdinand Porsche was born on September 3rd, 1875 in Maffersdorf, now Vratislavice, in the Czech Republic, where his father ran a plumbing business. From early childhood Ferdinand showed a great interest in electricity. His father dismissed this interest as foolish and encouraged Ferdinand to sign up for an apprenticeship in plumbing. When he was 18, and following a course of study at the Imperial Technical School, Porsche was hired by Bela Egger & Co. an electrical company. He soon became manager of the test room and, in 1897, developed an electric motor that was directly mounted to wheel hubs. It was the first of its kind. In the same year he joined k.u.k. Hofwagenfabrik Jacob Lohner & Co., in Vienna, in the newly inaugurated "Electric Motor Department." Three years later, in 1900, the Lohner-Porsche, a transmissionless car powered by Porsche electric motors mounted to the wheel hubs was introduced as a great innovation at the Paris World Exhibition.

In 1906, after eight years with Lohner, Porsche was hired as Technical Director by Austro-Daimler. While there, he participated in several races, winning the "Prinz-Heinrich-Fahrt" in 1910. In 1917 he was promoted to General Director and in 1922 he designed the "Sascha," a small racecar that managed to win the "Targa Florio." Among the numerous projects signed by Ferdinand Porsche during his tenure at Austro-Daimler were powerful aircraft engines, large locomotive engines, fire engines, trolleybuses and hybrid electric-gasoline transportation systems.

37 center *In 1910 Ferdinand Porsche won the "Prinz-Heinrich-Fahrt", the most famous reliability race of its time. He drove an Austro-Daimler.*

37 bottom *A project Ferdinand Porsche undertook for Lohner. He was one of the very first engineers to dedicate himself to the development of electric and hybrid vehicles.*

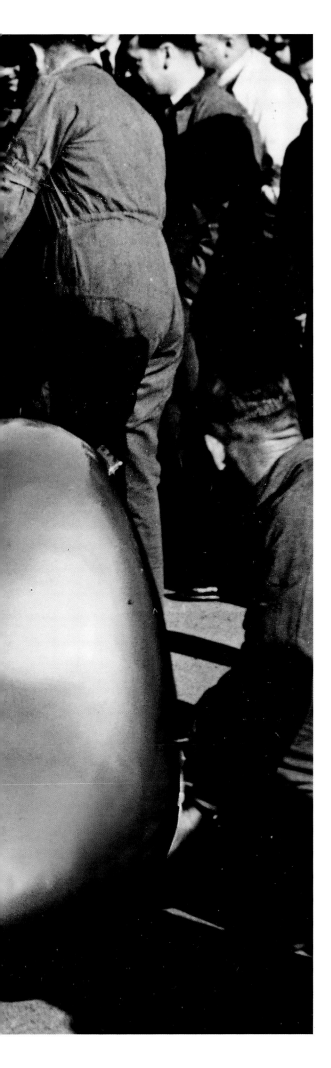

In 1923 Ferdinand Porsche became Technical Director and Administration Advisor of Daimler-Motoren-Gesellschaft in Stuttgart. Under his guidance the Mercedes Kompressorwagen was developed. In 1924 this car finished first overall in the Targa Florio. For this success, the Stuttgart Polytechnic conferred an honorary doctorate on Ferdinand Porsche. His Mercedes-Benz S, SS, and SSK models, equipped with supercharged engines were considered for years to come the epitome of the sport car and success in competition. In 1929 Ferdinand Porsche left Daimler-Benz and moved to Austria as Technical Director of Steyr-Werke AG.

A year and a half later, Ferdinand Porsche opened his own, independent design studio in Stuttgart. It was recorded in the Company Register on April 25th, 1931 as "Dr. Ing. h. c. F. Porsche GmbH, Konstruktionen und Beratung für Motoren und Fahrzeuge." On August 10th, 1931 the patent for torsion bar suspension was taken out. This alone would have sufficed to immortalize the name of Ferdinand Porsche in the automotive hall of fame. In 1932, commissioned by Auto Union, Porsche designed a Grand Prix single-seater equipped with a supercharged 16-cylinder engine for the new 750-kg (1650 lbs) class. The Auto Union Vehicle P (with the "P" standing for Porsche) won 32 of its 64 races, opening the door for drivers of the caliber of Hans Stuck and Bernd Rosemeyer to set a whole series of world records.

38-39 Bernd Rosemeyer in the Porsche-designed 1937 Auto Union Stromlinie Avus. Rosemeyer set numerous world speed records and competed in exhilarating races against Mercedes-Benz.

39 Ferdinand Porsche admires one of his masterpieces, the Auto Union Type C (also known as Porsche Project No. 22), which was equipped with a 16-cyclinder engine.

40 Ferdinand Porsche was one of the greatest automobile designers of all time.

41 Ferry (second from left) and Ferdinand Porsche (second from right) look over some technical drawings.

Following this, Ferdinand Porsche took on his most grandiose project to date which, the following year, resulted in his receiving the title of Honorary Professor. While at Austro-Daimler and Daimler-Benz he had already begun to think of a utilitarian car. Later, on June 22nd, 1934, an agreement for such a vehicle was announced between the Porsche Design Studio and the Association of Auto Industry of the Reich. This can fairly be said to be the official birth date of the Volkswagen better known as the Beetle. The cornerstone of the Volkswagen plant was laid down in 1938. In the years that followed, Ferdinand Porsche was one of the main managers of Volkswagen GmbH, but shortly before production was to start World War II broke out. The factory switched to war production and the Volkswagen was initially used as a platform for the development of the "Kübelwagen" and "Schwimmwagen" military vehicles. During the war the Design Studio developed the heavy armored tank "Maus" (Mouse) and the "Ostrad" tractor, as well as projects such as wind generators and the "Volkstraktor" (People's Tractor). In the fall of 1944 the Porsche Design Studio moved from Stuttgart to Gmünd in Carinthia (Austria).

At the end of 1945 Ferdinand Porsche was arrested and held captive for 22 months in various prisons. Upon his release, he oversaw the project for the Cisitalia race car; this was not a 356 as often incorrectly reported elsewhere. The single-seater was created by his son Ferry. After close examination he was of the following opinion, "I would not have changed one single screw."

Doctor Ferdinand Porsche died on January 30th, 1951, in Stuttgart, leaving his widow Aloisa Johanna Kaes, whom he married in 1903. A daughter Louise and son Ferdinand Anton Ernst, known as "Ferry," were born of this marriage. Louise later married the Viennese lawyer, Dr. Anton Piëch and, following his death in 1952, took over management of Porsche Konstruktionen GmbH, from which today's Porsche Holding in Austria originated.

42 *Ferdinand Porsche with his grandsons Ferdinand Piëch (right) and Ferdinand Alexander Porsche.*

After the war, Dr. Porsche's son Ferdinand Anton Ernst ("Ferry") Porsche, born on September 19th, 1909, capably guided the Design Studio with the right mix of entrepreneurial spirit through the transformation process that made Porsche one of the most well-known sports car makers in the world. He had been one of his father's first collaborators in the Design Studio he had founded in Stuttgart in 1931. After finishing his course of studies, Ferry Porsche held a year-long internship at Bosch, in Stuttgart, followed by a year of intense one-on-one training on the technical aspects of automobiles. By 1932 Ferry Porsche was already responsible for various aspects of the business, such as supervision of design, coordination of planning, and management of relations with such customers as the Auto Union of Zwickau. As far as the Volkswagen (known in-house as Type 60) was concerned, he was responsible for handling its road-testing program.

Following detention and subsequent internment for numerous months at the hands of American and French allied forces, Ferry Porsche returned to Gmünd, in Carinthia, in July 1946, taking over management of the business, while his father was still a prisoner of the French. The realization of his idea for a small sports car based on the Volkswagen, developed together with the head designer Karl Rabe (1895-1968) and body designer Erwin Komenda (1904-1966) came seventeen years after his father had first opened the design studio. This marked a decisive turn for the company, which from that point onwards gradually lost its character as a studio exclusively concerned with design, to one that was also in the business of production. Then, in 1948, with the Porsche 356, Ferry Porsche laid the foundation for the company's worldwide fame as a producer of successful sports cars and racecars. He adopted his father's design ideas for the Volkswagen (rear-mounted, air-cooled boxer engine) and also followed in the competitive tradition his father had always focused on from his early design days in 1900.

Fifty-two units of the 356 were hand made in Gmünd. In 1949 Ferry Porsche returned to Stuttgart-Zuffenhausen to take over again as Managing Director. The buildings they had previously occupied, however, had by then been taken over by Americans. The first Porsche 356, consequently, was built in precarious circumstances in spaces that were rented from the

43 *Ferry Porsche and his most important creation—the 356. It was Ferry who transformed Porsche into one of the greatest names in sports cars manufacturing.*

Reutter bodyworks in the spring of 1950. An agreement, which would later reveal itself farsighted as far as the company's destiny was concerned, was made between Ferry Porsche and Heinz Nordhoff (1899–1968), the managing director of Volkswagen. According to the terms of the agreement, Volkswagen would provide all the necessary parts for production of the sports car. Moreover, cars produced by the company would be marketed by the network of Volkswagen dealerships, who would also provide technical assistance. The contracts Ferry Porsche drew up with the main Volkswagen dealerships were the second central pillar he secured for the company, guaranteeing the financial stability it would need for future developments.

When his father died in 1951, Ferry Porsche shouldered responsibility for the entire company, guiding it as Managing Director to its transformation from a private limited partnership to public limited company in 1972. Ferry Porsche continued to play a deciding role in the advancement of the Porsche spirit even as President of the Supervisory Board. In 1990 Ferry Porsche resigned from that position, but remained a part of the board, as Honorary President, until his death in Zell am See on March 27th, 1998.

In 1972, in response to power struggles among their children (and there were many of them…), Ferry Porsche and his sister Louise Piëch decided that, after them, no other member of the family should work in the family business. The founder's grandchildren, Ferdinand Piëch, Planning Director, Hans-Peter Porsche, Production Director, and Ferdinand Alexander Porsche, who was responsible for design, all left the company. The company name was changed in the same year from Dr. Ing. h. c. F. Porsche KG to Porsche AG. The new managing director, essentially Ferry Porsche's successor, was Ernst Fuhrmann. Ordinary shares, nevertheless, remained in the hands of the Piëch and Porsche families. In 1992 Wendelin Wiedeking was nominated Chairman of the Board of Directors and, between 1993 and 2009 served as President and CEO of the company. The fiscal year 1994/1995 saw a return to profitability and since then the firm has grown to become the most profitable auto company in the world. Today Porsche belongs entirely to Volkswagen AG.

44 Fritz Huschke von Hanstein (standing), a Prussian aristocrat (1911–1996), was also a good race driver, and later became the legendary director of Porsche's racing department.

The Early Races

The very first vehicle to display the Porsche badge was made in Gmünd in 1948 and was a sports car designed for both road *and* track. Its aerodynamically designed shape was based on the pre-war racecar that ran in the Berlin–Rome race and its prototype served as the test car for future competitions. No sooner had the 356 left the drawing board, than it was entered in a competition. In 1951 Porsche took out a patent on its synchromesh gearbox, which made gear shifting smoother in everyday driving and faster in competitive driving. The same year Porsche had its first victory in its class at Le Mans with an aluminum body 356 Coupe. It produced 46 hp, and reached a top speed of 99 mph (160 km/h). The 24 Hours, at that time, were really long hours…

The commitment shown by numerous private racing drivers pushed Porsche to start participating actively in car races. Thus, the Porsche 550 was born, and immediately won its first race, in 1953, on the Nürburgring circuit. The era of racing cars had begun at Porsche. In the 550, the 4-cylinder boxer engine was mounted in front of the rear axle, a configuration that made the spyder especially agile. A 5-speed gearbox was used for the first time. In addition, the racing division engineers modified the cylinder heads in such a way as to make it possible to equip them with two sparkplugs each. This sped up and improved combustion resulting in improved power output and efficiency. That year the 550 Coupe, which was still equipped with the classic pushrod engine was entered in the race. The engine's 78 hp had to propel 1,213 lbs (550 kg) and it won in its class again. The same happened in 1954, this time with a four-camshaft engine and about 110 hp. Success was repeated in 1955.

The year 1956 marked the Le Mans debut of the 356 A whose absolute victory at the Targa Florio, with Umberto Maglioli alone at the wheel, had been sensational. With the 550 A Spyder, Porsche made a noteworthy technical advance. A tubular space frame replaced the previous model's ladder frame, making the car much more rigid and 88 lbs (40 kg) lighter with a total weight of 1,213 lbs (550 kg). The 1.5-liter Fuhrmann engine produced 135 hp, and the running gear was completely rethought. With an overwhelming victory in its own class, and fifth place overall, Porsche proved that the little 550 A Coupe could excel not only on the mountain roads of Sicily, but also on the race circuits with their higher average speeds.

45 top Max Nathan and Gert Kaiser in a 356 Porsche at the 1956 Mille Miglia. The Mille Miglia was one of the few famous races Porsche never managed to win.

45 bottom The light version of the Porsche 356 Coupé making its first appearance at the 24 Hours of Le Mans. Auguste Veuillet, chief importer of Porsches to France at the time, is at the wheel with his co-pilot, Edmonde Mouche.

46-47 Solitude-Rennen 1956: Hans Hermann at the wheel of the 550 A Spyder (number 10), Richard von Frankenberg in the Type 645 "Mickey Mouse" (number 11) and, farther back, with number 30, Max Nathan in a 550 Spyder.

48 top Hans Hermann in a 550 Spyder at the 1954 Carrera Panamericana. He won third place overall and first in class, dominating the decidedly more powerful competition.

48 bottom The Porsche 550 (also known as the 1500 RS) was developed from a 356 platform and was produced from 1953 until 1957, both in coupé and open versions. The model name, by the way, was based on the project number, not on the vehicle's weight (550 kg).

49 The 550/550 A was powered by the 'Fuhrmann engine' (Type 547), an air-cooled, four-cylinder boxer, with four overhead camshafts driven by countershafts, double injection with a dual-plug ignition system that used twin distributors and twin-choke carburetors.

In 1957 the 550 Spyder underwent changes to evolve into the 718 Spyder, which then went on to become an excellent competition car not only for private racers, but for the company as well. It wasn't until 1958, however, that all expectations were fully met with the arrival of the 718 RSK. The Porsches that were equipped with Fuhrmann engines whose capacity was increased to 1.6 liters turned out to be extremely fast, to the point of being a concern even for the Ferrari, Jaguar, and Aston racing cars with their three liter engines. After 24 hours of racing at Le Mans, triumph was complete. The Behra/Hermann car crossed the finish line with third place overall, directly followed by the Barth/Frère duo. These results represented victory in both the 1.5-liter and 2.0-liter classes, while the overall team victory was the perfect crowning of a perfect weekend. In 1959, on the other hand, none of the cars entered in the competition managed to finish.

In 1960 it was the turn of the 718 Spyder RS60; it took first place, overall, at Sebring and in the Targa Florio. The aerodynamics of the RS60 differed from those on the earlier model. It featured coil spring rear suspension and the now obligatory luggage compartment behind the engine. Another interesting vehicle, the 356B 1600 GS Carrera GTL Abarth was also entered at Le Mans that year. This car's body, a lighter version of the 356 B, was produced by Zagato thanks to the mediation of Carlo Abarth. The 1600 GS weighed 220 lbs (100 kg) less than the 356 B. Development of the 718 continued in 1961 with the 718 RS61, which was produced in several versions and with several different engines, including a 2-liter (185 hp), and a 1.6-liter (160 hp). In 1962 the 718 W-RS Spyder made its debut at Le Mans with its eight-cylinder, two-liter engine with 210 hp and a top speed of 174 mph (280 km/h).

50 top Hans Hermann driving a 718 RS60 in the Rossfeld mountain race. Hermann, born in 1928, gave Porsche its first Le Mans victory in 1970.

50 bottom Hans Hermann exchanges a few words with Vic Elford. They were two of Porsche's most successful drivers of all time, earning victories both at Le Mans and in the Targa Florio.

51 The 1000 kilometer race at Nürburgring, 1959. Hans Hermann in the 718 RSK speaks with Huschke von Hanstein, director of Porsche's racing department at the time.

52-53 top The 718 was a prime example of Porsche's philosophy of constantly reworking its racecars over the years. The lightest versions barely weighed 990 lbs (450 kg).

52-53 bottom The Porsche 718 was based on the 550 and was built in a number of versions between 1957 and 1962. Several underwent key modifications and even competed in Formula 1 and Formula 2 races.

53 bottom The first 718s still had to make do with a 1.5-liter engine with not much more than 140 hp. Over the course of the years, however, power was upgraded to 240 hp.

54 top Hans Hermann again, still in a 718 RS 60 Spyder, here he's at Sebring in 1960.

As a sideline, Porsche decided to enter the Formula 1 class adventure as well. In 1961 it entered the single-seater, 1.5-liter (190-hp) 787 in the race and, with Dan Gurney at the wheel, took third place in the World Championship. Matters improved in 1962 thanks to the Type 804 (eight cylinders, 1.5-liter and still approximately 190 hp), which enabled Dan Gurney to win the French Grand Prix.

In 1964 the pace quickened when the Porsches that carried type numbers beginning with the famous number 9 made their debut in the racing world. The first of these was the fabulous 904 Carrera GTS, the first Porsche to have an especially light, plastic body, bonded to a steel space frame. The 904 Carrera GTS was powered by a four-cylinder, two-liter engine, derived from the Carrera 2 and could produce up to 180 hp. There was also an eight-cylinder version (904/8), equipped with a Formula 1 engine, with about 260 hp. Starting in 1965, the 904/6 was added with the six-cylinder, two-liter engine of the 911 producing approximately 200 hp.

54 bottom The Porsche 904 was the heir to the 718. It was designed by "Butzi" Porsche and was produced between 1963 and 1965. It had originally been planned as a road-going car. However, in-house it was understood right from the start that it would be used primarily as a racecar.

55 Colin Davis and Antonio Pucci, official drivers for Porsche, won the Targa Florio in 1964 at the wheel of a Porsche 904 GTS. The vehicle wasn't just good to look at, it was really fast, too.

In 1966 Porsche set up a new racing department. Its first product was the 906, also known as the Carrera 6. For private race team customers this was powered by the modified 911 engine, but for the official team was equipped with an eight-cylinder (Type 711) that developed 260 hp. It weighed about 1,433 lbs (650 kg). In 1967 the 910, the direct successor to the 906, and the 907, a further evolution of the still-relatively new 910, were produced. The 907 was the first Porsche ever to reach an average speed of more than 124 mph (200 km/h) at Le Mans.

In 1968 the World Manufacturers' Championship called for prototype cars with three-liter engines and sports cars with up to five-liter engines. Porsche designed the 908, with an eight-cylinder, 3-liter boxer engine and up to 370 hp. In the struggle for overall victory, however, Porsche could not compete against the higher-powered Ford GT40s, even if in the qualifiers Siffert/Herrmann attained pole position for the Porsche 908 and in doing so highlighted the vehicle's potential.

In 1969 Porsche failed to win the overall title at the 24 Hours of Le Mans, but did win a myriad of class victories. The German stable of racers seemed to be destined for victory in the Targa Florio. After first place in 1956, victories followed in 1959, 1960, 1963, 1964, 1966 through to 1970 and one final win in 1973.

56 In 1969 Porsche won a quadruple victory with the 908/02 at the Targa Florio. Gerhard Mitter and Udo Schütz were the overall winners.

56-57 The Porsche 906, which came with either a six- or eight-cylinder engine (906 and 906/8) was officially introduced as a street car. It was produced between 1965 and 1966, but managed to win numerous races into the early 1970s.

Porsche at Le Mans

Le Mans, June 15th, 1969. Less than four hours to go before the end of the race. Vic Elford and Richard Atwood, at the wheel of the new Porsche 917 'Long Tail', were well ahead of the field. The previous year's winners, Jacky Ickx and Jackie Oliver, driving the Ford GT40, were still a good 6 laps behind. Then, all of a sudden, a malfunction of the clutch put and end to the victorious gallop of the new racecar with its 4.5-liter, twelve-cylinder engine. The second 917, driven by Rolf Stommelen and Kurt Ahrens and fastest in training, had already dropped out ten hours into the race because of a malfunctioning clutch. But excitement in the Porsche pits didn't end here. Hans Herrmann and Gérard Larrousse were writing one of the most exciting chapters in the history of Le Mans. In the first phase of the race their 908 'Long Tail' lost 35 minutes due to a problem with one of the wheel bearings. After a furious, twenty-hour pursuit the French-German duo managed to reach the vehicle in the lead, the Ford GT40 of Ickx/Oliver.

58-59 A 917 K won the 1970 24 Hours of Daytona with Pedro Rodriguez, Leo Kinnunen and Brian Redman at the wheel. By the end of the race, the number 2 had a 45-lap advantage over the number 1, also a Porsche 917, driven by Brian Redman. A 917 K won Le Mans in 1970 and 1971 as well.

In the final stretch the two cars were neck and neck, each taking the lead a number of times. Hermann, however, failed to take advantage of the better braking performance of his light Porsche because a warning light on the dashboard had lit up, informing him the brake pads were worn out. As a result, Icks crossed the finish line with an advantage just shy of 394 feet (120 meters). To make matters worse, it was later found that the warning light was defective and the brake system had been working perfectly. It was another 24 Hours of Le Mans without a Porsche victory, despite the huge expectations.

Numerology has always been part of the Porsche tradition. The sequence 9-1-7 denotes one of the most legendary cars ever to have been run on any race circuit worldwide. It is the symbol of a whole generation of racers. Its triumphs were interrupted only by the introduction of new regulations, not by any stronger competition. One of the most important people to have been involved in its development was a young engineer by the name of Ferdinand Piëch.

60-61 This Porsche 917/20 is a very unique vehicle, not only because of its color, which earned it the nickname "Pink Pig," but also because it is the only vehicle which blends elements of the short- and long-tailed 917. Its racing success, however, was slow in coming.

61 Steve McQueen chatting with Juan Fangio during the filming of his movie "Le Mans" in which, of course, Porsches played the lead roles.

At the end of 1967, when the new regulations for the Sports-Prototype World Championship were introduced, Porsche decided to design a new racecar for the 5.0-liter class – the 917. This car was the descendant of the 907 and 908 models, both multiple victors. Initially the 917 was equipped with a 4.5-liter twelve-cylinder engine which delivered 560 hp at 8,300 rpm, very powerful for those times. With all that power, the 917 was touching speeds of 249 mph (400 km/h) creating a real challenge for the Weissach team of aerodynamics engineers.

The final contest was in 1970. Seven Porsche 917s were lined up against eleven Ferrari 512s, not to mention the team of fast prototype class cars equipped with three-liter Formula 1 engines that were trying for the jackpot. In the end, instead, it was the red and white no. 23, 917 'Short Tail' of the Salzburg team that gave the Stuttgart-Zuffenhausen car maker its first overall win. The vehicle was barely 36 in. (92 cm) high and had an aluminum trellis frame covered with an ultra-thin plastic body. Hans Hermann and Richard Attwood took turns at the wheel. The twelve-cylinder still had a 4.5-liter engine and delivered 580 hp. Second place went to the 917 'Long Tail', driven by Gérard Larrousse and Willi Kauhsen. This car's body was painted in a 1970s palette of psychedelic colors and entered the annals of automobile racing as the "Hippie Car." In 1970, with seven overall victories already under its belt, all won by the now-dominant 917, Porsche also won the Sportscar World Championship.

Scenes for the film "Le Mans," which opened in theaters a year later, on June 23rd, 1971, were shot on site during and after the 1970 Le Mans race. Even today this film is considered the most legendary movie about automobile racing of all time. The camera-car in which Steve McQueen, the main character, took second place at Sebring was the 908/02.

In 1971 Porsche set a number of records at Le Mans. Of 49 cars at the starting lineup, 33 carried the Porsche badge, a first that has yet to be beaten. For this race, Porsche had honed the aerodynamics of the 917. Its efforts paid off. During the preliminary tests, Derek Bell reached an unofficial speed of 246 mph (396 km/h) on the long straight at the wheel of a 'Long Tail'. Jackie Oliver completed a test lap at an average speed of 155.637 mph (250.475 km/h) and, at the end of the long straight recorded a top speed of 240 mph (386 km/h). Helmut Marko and Gijs van Lennep took first place with a Porsche 917 'Short Tail', covering 397 laps for a total of 3315.09 miles (5,335.13 kilometers) at an average speed of 138.133 mph (222.304 km/h). This record remained unbeaten for 39 years.

In their triumphant ride this duo also won the "Index of Performance" for the best performance based on fuel consumption. The 917's career, however, was abruptly interrupted following implementation of the new regulations at Le Mans, introduced specifically to check Porsche dominance.

To make up for this, another version of the 917 was eliminating the competition elsewhere. Porsche had already participated in the American CanAm championship in 1969 with the 917 PA (Porsche-Audi), which in fact hadn't a chance of winning. Following this defeat, different ways of increasing the power output had been looked at, and a sixteen-cylinder engine had been mounted on three different units, all of which were used as test-cars. Then, in 1971, Porsche began to use twin turbochargers, making it possible to upgrade the power output to about 850 hp. Finally, in 1973 they produce the 917/30. This was a 5.4-liter, twin-turbocharged, 1,100 hp engine with a maximum torque of 810 lb.-ft. (1,098 Nm) at 6,400 rpm. The vehicle weighed 1,863 lbs (845 kg), accelerated from 0 to 62 mph (0 to 100 km/h) in 2.4 seconds and could reach a speed of 186 mph (300 km/h) in 11.3 seconds. This twelve-cylinder was perhaps the most powerful engine to ever have been raced on circuits. Not to be overlooked is the fact that, on the test bench, it had reached 1,570 hp.

62 bottom Hans Herrmann and Richard Atwood at the wheel of the Salzburg Porsche team's number 23, the legendary Porsche 917 KH. They were the first to cross the finish line of the 1970 24 Hours of Le Mans. This was Porsche's first overall win in this legendary endurance classic.

62-63 In 1970, on the occasion of its first Le Mans victory, the Porsche 917's 4.9-liter V12 developed 600 hp at 8,400 rpm and a maximum torque of 405 ft.-lb. (549 Nm) at 6,000 rpm. The vehicle, weighing only 1,764 lbs (800 kg), reached a top speed of almost 240 mph (390 km/h).

64-65 The Martini Racing team's Porsche 917 K that, with its number 22, dominated the 1971 24 Hours of Le Mans.

During this period the key word was - turbo. The first racecar in a 24 Hours of Le Mans to be equipped with an exhaust gas turbocharger was the 911 Carrera RSR Turbo 2.1. This was in 1974. With this very powerful evolution of the 911, Porsche prepared for its 1975 debut in the World Championship for production cars. Its six-cylinder boxer engine was downsized to 2.1 liters (2,142 cc) to comply with regulations and thanks to an intercooler exchanger developed about 500 hp. The engine had a magnesium crankcase, while the piston rods and intake valves were made of titanium. During its long experience in the United States with the 917/10, before the introduction of the 917/30, Porsche had accumulated plenty of know-how on exhaust gas turbocharger technology. This was still a fairly new technology as applied to high performance gasoline engines. Porsche became so well versed in the management of the supercharging pressure from the exhaust gas, that it could handle using it in competitions. An amusing anecdote. In the 1974 Le Mans the 911 Carrera RSR Turbo 2.1 was in second place behind a Matra, when the latter was forced to stop to deal with a gearbox problem. Porsche sent two of its best mechanics, experts in transmissions, to the French pits to help them repair it. They fixed the gearbox of their strong competitor in a record 20 minutes. And then? The Matra won the race. The reason for this strange involvement in the emergency repair wasn't difficult to guess. It was Porsche who had designed the Matra's transmission.

In 1976 Porsche arrived at Le Mans with two new cars. Jacky Ikxs and Gijs van Lennep won the top spot on the podium at the wheel of a Porsche 936 equipped with the well-tried 2.1-liter turbo boxer engine which by this time developed 550 hp. Thanks to this victory, the Stuttgart vehicle set two more records. It was the first victory at Le Mans for a boxer engine and it was also the first victory for an exhaust-gas turbocharged engine. Since it met the technical requirements of Group 6 for the Sportscar World Championship, the 936 was, for all intents and purposes, a racecar with a mid-mounted engine and trellis frame. It weighed barely 1,687 lbs (765 kg).

66 Jacky Ickx and Gijs van Lennep won the 24 Hours of Le Mans at the wheel of a Porsche 936 powered by a 2.1-liter, 520-hp, boxer engine with a single turbocharger (starting in 1977 this combination was upgraded to twin turbochargers and 540 hp).

66-67 The 936/80 was raced by the Joest Racing team in the 1980 24 Hours of Le Mans, where it finished second. It developed 580 hp (with a 2.1-liter boxer engine) and was slightly longer than the previous version.

The 935 made its Le Mans debut in 1976 alongside the 936 and was successful as well. The car, a descendant of the 911 Turbo (930) was entered in Group 5 of the World Championship for Makes. This racing version of the 911 weighed 2,138 lbs (970 kg). Under the hood there was a 2.8-liter turbo engine which Porsche claimed developed "at least 590 hp." Porsche won again in 1977 with a 936 Spyder that raced the last few miles with a deactivated cylinder. In 1978 the "Moby Dick," or rather a 911 officially known as 935/78, was entered for the first time. Its rear-mounted, 3.2-liter turbo engine with 850 hp was the first to be equipped with water-cooled four-valve cylinder heads. The first and only vehicle with a rear-mounted engine to score an overall victory at Le Mans was the 935 K3 of the Kremer Racing Team, with Klaus Ludwig and Don and Bill Whittington at the wheel in 1979. This was also the first overall victory at Le Mans for a private Porsche team.

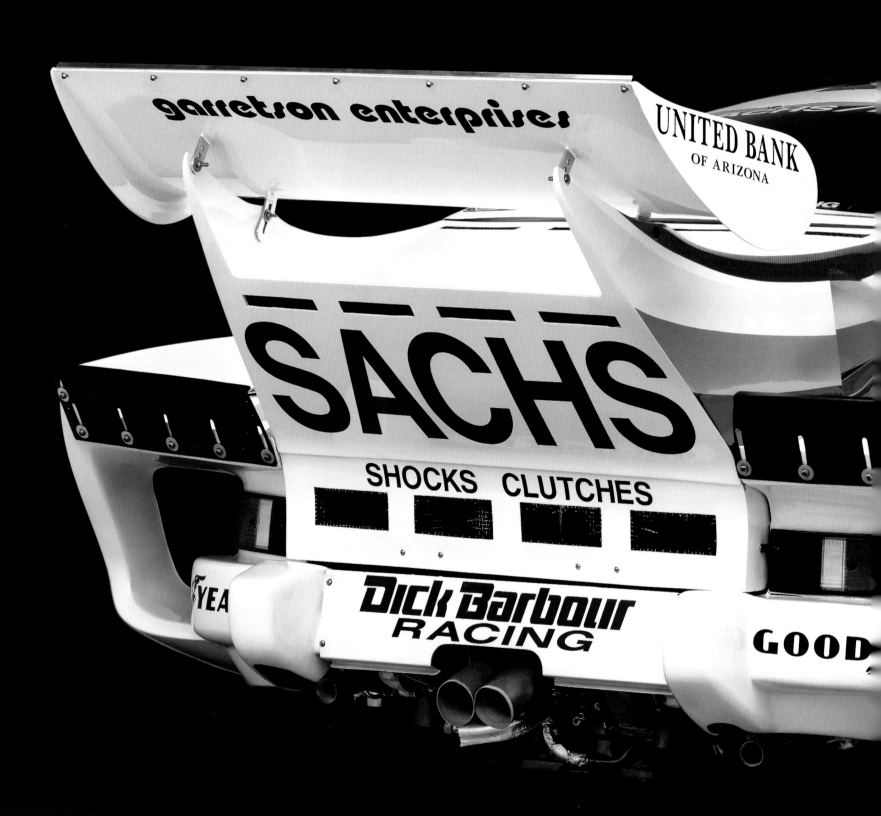

In 1980 Porsche finished empty-handed at Le Mans. But it did introduce the 924 Carrera GT that year, the sportiest version of the 924 with rear transaxle. This was also the first track appearance of a Porsche equipped with a water-cooled front-mounted engine.

In 1981 Peter W. Schutz, the new Porsche CEO, was determined to win another victory and had the racing division pull the 936s that had won in 1977 and 1978 from the displays of the Porsche museum. The regulations at that time did allow vehicles with high-capacity turbo engines so the racing department equipped the 936s with the twin-turbo, 2.65-liter engine intended for one-seaters in Indianapolis. This engine had never before been entered in a race. At Le Mans the six-cylinder developed about 620 hp and won. This success marked the beginning of a whole series of back to back victories.

68-69 A Porsche 935 K3 raced in 1980. It was powered by a 3.1-liter boxer coupled with two turbochargers and developed 680 hp. Kerb weight was approx. 2,200 lbs (1,000 kg).

Racing Supremacy

70-71 top In 1985 Stuck/Bell's number 2 Porsche 962 C came in third at the 24 Hours of Le Mans.

70-71 bottom A number of versions of the Porsche 962 were raced between 1984 and 1991, but they were almost always equipped with a 2.9-liter six-cylinder boxer engine that developed 680 hp and brought it to top speeds of about 249 mph (400 km/h).

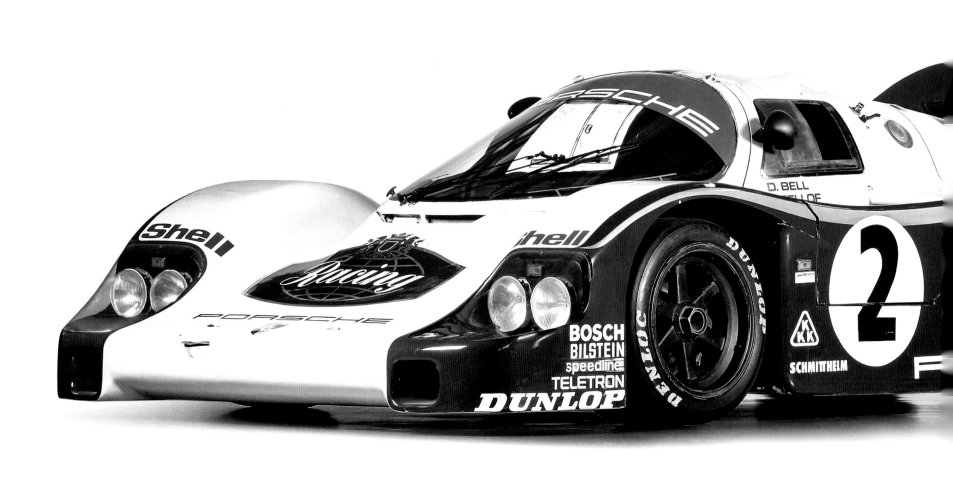

On March 27th, 1982 a revolutionary racecar made the first rounds of the test track in Weissach. It was the Porsche 956. Designed to meet the new technical requirements for "Group C," it was the first Weissach racecar to be made with an aluminum monocoque chassis. Its bodywork was revolutionary in the racecar world. Its inverted wing section side pods and the flat undertray were designed to create the ground effect needed to keep the car glued to the ground. After much research, Porsche had applied a Formula 1 principle to generate downforce and adapted it for use on sports cars. The car weighed 1,764 lbs (800 kg), as per the regulations, and was powered by the same engine that had powered the 936 which won the 24 Hours of Le Mans in 1981. It was an upgraded 2.65-liter that developed 620 hp. On June 20th, 1982 Porsche celebrated a triple victory but the best was still to come. In the following year the Porsche 956 took nine out of the top ten positions, including the first eight. No other car and no other brand had ever been so successfully dominant in the world's

72-73 In all, Porsche produced about 90 units of the 962. In the eight years between 1984 and 1991 it won approximately 54 victories and numerous championships. Not surprisingly, the 962 is considered one of the most successful racecars of all time.

73 In 1986 nine of the top ten finishers at Le Mans were Porsches, with a 962 C in the lead. The most exciting aspect that year, however, was probably Porsche's experimentation with new technology, like the first use of a dual-clutch on an official 962 C.

The 956 won once again in 1985, even if that year it was officially called the 962 C. The front axle centerline was moved forward by 4.7 in. (12 cm) to make the car eligible under the IMSA regulations. Extension of the wheelbase to 9 feet (2.77 m), also involved modification of the front overhang and made it necessary to review the aerodynamics of the whole car. Because of the regulation-mandated narrower tires, the area beneath the car available for creating the air flow ground effect was increased by 2 in. (5 cm). During qualifying, Porsche went for a three-liter turbo that developed about 700 hp, which enabled Hans-Joachim Stuck to set the Le Mans track record for the fastest lap. His 3:14.80 minutes correspond to an average speed of 156.471 mph (251.815 km/h). The next win was Porsche's tenth overall victory at Le Mans, which meant the score was now even with Ferrari.

Porsche continued to dominate Le Mans without interruption. In 1986 it filled nine of the first ten positions in the qualifiers with a 962 C occupying the top step of the podium. In the meantime, these victories started to be taken almost for granted and attention was turned to technical innovations. That year, for example, Porsche first experimented with a dual-clutch transmission, trying it out on a vehicle that was officially designated a 962 C. Porsche also raced a 961, which was the racing version of the 959, but was basically a mobile test bench. This sporty, high-performance 961 had already come in first, second, and sixth in the January 1986 Paris–Dakar Rally, thereby proving its power and reliability. Its use in competition highlighted the higher performance delivered by the latest technical advances. Later these technological advances would be introduced on road cars as well, starting out with the 959. In the 961 these advances consisted of a twin turbo, all-wheel drive, the differential slip of the 2.85-liter engine, a six-speed gearbox and brake calipers. The six-speed gearbox was identical to the one that later came as a standard feature on the 959. The engine, which was more or less the same as the one that later became standard in the 959, developed 640 hp, almost 200 hp more than the road version. This was thanks to the pressure boost from the supercharging, the optimization of the intercooler and a new mapping of the central control unit.

In 1987 Porsche won again with a 962 C. In 1988 a Jaguar won, but eight 962 C Porsches finished in the Top Ten. These were transitional years for Porsche, because in 1987 the Weissach team had begun developing and testing an engine and body

for a single-seater to be raced in the American Championship Auto Racing Teams (CART).

This venture which involved considerable effort on their part in 1988, 1989, 1990 and 1991. As a result, Porsche didn't finish first at Le Mans (in 1991 a Mazda with a Wankel engine and Porsche gearbox won...). Porsche attention was focused entirely on the CART and then Formula 1. 1993 was the final year for Group C at Le Mans and therefore the last year a 962 could participate. But the serial winner didn't leave Le Mans for long ...

In 1994 new technical regulations introduced new categories. In order of increasing performance these included Le Mans Prototypes, Le Mans GT1s and Le Mans GT2s. Following close scrutiny of the technical requirements for the GT1 category, and discovery of a loophole, the Porsche engineers figured out that, with a few modifications, the 962 could actually be homologated as a Le Mans GT1, since the road-going version, the Dauer 962, was already homologated. The Dauer 962 LM-GT had a flat undertray, narrower tires, and weighed 2,204 lbs (1,000 kg), the minimum requirement.

Porsche aimed to win the GT1 category, but ended up achieving instead its 13th overall win at Le Mans. This race also marked the first time Porsche used xenon headlights.

74-75 The "Holbert Racing Löwenbrau Special" is one of the most famous 962s. The 962-103, produced in September 1984, was one of the first 962s and, in the course of its long career, won 15 races. In 2011 the vehicle was auctioned off for almost 2 million dollars.

75 One of a kind. The racing version of the 959, known as the 961. This race-going test bench won a noteworthy seventh place at the 1986 Le Mans.

In 1996 and 1997 the private, very professional, team of Reinhold Joest won the 24 Hours of Le Mans with a WSC Spyder. This was a car originally designed for use in races in the United States but, following an abrupt change in the regulations, Porsche had decided to interrupt its production. The team owner, Reinhold Joest, took over one of the Porsche prototypes and personally paid the Weissach engineers to rework its aerodynamics and suspension systems for the race. In this way, a second WSC Spyder was developed at Weissach. Both of the vehicle prototypes had a carbon fiber monocoque, with carbon-fiber-reinforced plastic sub frames, and a flat undertray in compliance with regulations. The engine was an old acquaintance: the twin turbo, six cylinder that had won the 962 C infinite victories. Its engine, which at the time developed 540 hp, would prove to be a determining factor in the vehicle's successive victories not only because of its power, but also because of the fine-tuning to ensure maximum efficiency. Even its tire friendly running gear turned out to be ideal for Le Mans. The WSC Spyder could race with one set of tires for longer than all the other competitors. The car's evolution, too, moved at a racing pace. In February it was decided that the Joest Racing team would participate in Le Mans. In May, a week before

the preliminary tests on the La Sarthe circuit, the last set of pre-season tests was conducted at Le Castellet, in the south of France. In these tests, the WSC Spyder was on equal footing with the competition. In the race itself, however, the number 7 WSC Spyder was unbeatable. In 1997 it ran again as number 7 with the same final result. In 1996 another significant debut took place, that of the 911 GT1, the first 911 to have a mid-mounted engine.

76-77 The 962-103 was the only vehicle to ever win the 24 Hours of Le Mans in two consecutive years, in 1986 and 1987. The same vehicle came in second in this race in 1985.

In 1998 Porsche took first and second place at Le Mans with its rolling test bench, the 911 GT1. After the first 911-derived mid-mounted engine vehicles that had been raced in the 1996 and 1997 Le Mans, the 1998 Porsche 911 GT1 held the interim position as the climax of classic sports car evolution in competition. Its 3.2-liter six-cylinder developed 600 hp, thanks to the twin turbochargers, while the updated central control unit transformed the high-performance engine into a master of fuel-consumption efficiency, a definite advantage at Le Mans. 1998 was also the first year when carbon brake disks were used on an official racing car. The 15-inch (380-mm) disks were combined with eight-piston calipers on the front axle and six-piston calipers at the rear. The front end of the previous 911 GT1 and 911 GT1 EVO models had still been made of sheet steel, but the 1998 GT1 had a carbon fiber monocoque and plastic bodywork. In its racing layout this Porsche weighed 2,138 lbs (970 kg). Homologation regulations required that a racecar should exist as a road car version. Porsche made this one, too, like the racecar version, with an extremely light and resistant carbon-fiber frame, which was subjected to the obligatory crash-test and passed with flying colors. A small series of these cars, limited to 21 units, was subsequently made for racecar driving enthusiasts. For the time being, the 1998 victory at Le Mans remains Porsche's last overall victory.

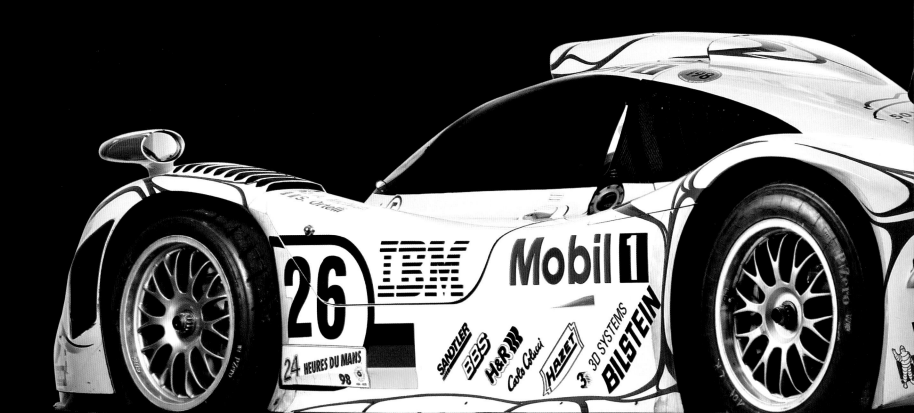

78-79 and 79 Officially, this car is called the Porsche 911 GT1, but it doesn't have much in common with the 911, especially given the fact that it is powered by a mid-mounted, water-cooled engine instead of the classic rear-mounted, air-cooled one.

80-81 Car number 26 won the 1998 Le Mans 24 Hours with Aiello/McNish/Ortelli at the wheel. The GT1 was pretty much at the end of its career that year, the Mercedes was certainly faster in all the other races but, at Le Mans, what counts most is reliability.

Porsche 356

It all begin with a Volkswagen Beetle. According to official documents, plans relating to the development of the first sports car called Porsche began on July 17th, 1947, and were based on a homemade steel trellis frame and Beetle running gear. Even the original engine was based on the Beetle's, but with a cubic capacity of 1.1 liters. It delivered not only 25 hp at 3,300 rpm, but also a handsome 35 hp at 4,000 rpm. The VW engine was mounted crossways but the Porsche, by contrast, had the engine mounted longitudinally, in front of the rear axle. The 356/1 model, therefore, had a mid-engine layout and its design bore all the hall marks of Erwin Komenda's mastery. The Roadster, weighing barely 1,290 lbs (585 kg) (the frame consisted of aluminum panels shaped using wooden patterns), made its maiden road trip on June 8th, 1948, attaining a top speed of 87 mph (140 km/h). The first Porsche with the frame number 356 001 and engine number 356-2-034969 was sold in Switzerland on the same day.

The buyer was a certain Rupprecht von Senger who bought it for the exorbitant price of 7,000 German marks (about 20,600 GBP). In the summer of 1947, when Ferry Porsche first floated the idea of developing his own sports cars for export to Switzerland, von Senger had already secured the rights to the first five. In addition to paying an advance for the option on an additional fifty cars, von Senger also funded production of the Porsches, facilitating the availability of spare parts, tires, and light alloy sheets throughout Switzerland. Legend has it that he smuggled in spark plugs in his trouser pockets because these were practically impossible to find in Germany in the aftermath of the war. On the occasion of the Swiss Grand Prix on July 4th, 1948, Rupprecht von Senger made his Porsche available to a group of select journalists. Just three days later the article "The Birth of a Great Name" was published in the Swiss magazine "Automobil Revue."

82-83 A 1954 Porsche 356. From the very beginning the 356 was appreciated as a racing car by amateur racers who often took it upon themselves to make changes to the vehicle in order to reduce its weight (for example, by eliminating the bumpers).

84 Production of a 356 engine in the late '50s: everything is handcrafted with great intensity and German precision.

The relationship with Switzerland continued to strengthen. Bernhard Blank, a car dealer and hotel owner from Zurich who Ferry Porsche had come to know through von Senger, transformed part of his hotel space into a showroom. In the winter of 1948 the first Porsche 356/2 Coupe was exhibited there. At that time, the plan was to build an additional 50 to 100 cars. Eventually 78,000 were built. Bernhard Blank also saw to it that the new car maker attended the March 1949 Geneva Auto Show, where the 356/2 Type model, with a body designed by Beutler of Thun, was first presented to an international audience. The car quickly became well known and was in great demand among automobile fans, especially in Switzerland, Sweden, and Austria. By the end of 1949, twenty-seven, each handcrafted, had been sold. The initial actual contractual sale made by the Swiss importer Blank in the spring of 1949 was the first Porsche 356/2 Cabriolet. The buyer was one Jolanda Tschudi, a young lady of the Zurich bourgeoisie, who thus became the world's first Porsche customer.

The very first Porsche prototype, 356 No.1, also went to Switzerland, to a woman customer of the name Elisabeth Spielhofer. She in turn, sold it to another woman, Rosemarie Muff, clearly someone with a taste for the finer things in life. In 1958 this car, No.1, was returned to Stuttgart-Zuffenhausen by Porsche itself, to be displayed in its own beautiful museum.

In the meantime the short-lived relationship with the Swiss hotelier Blank had cooled and came to an end. But the connection with Switzerland did not end there. It was the Swiss company Amag, the next importer of Porsches to Switzerland, who first published Porsche advertisements worldwide.

85 top Assembly of the 356 B. By the end of the fifties, 32 units were produced per day.

85 bottom An engine is installed in a 356 B sometime around 1960. The process was referred to as the 'marriage' and, at the time, was mostly a manual activity.

86 top   Ferry Porsche in a Porsche 356 A Cabriolet, on the occasion of the inaugural of a bust of his father, Ferdinand Porsche, at the Volkswagen plant/headquarters in Wolfsburg. The year is 1955, but the vehicle is from model-year 1956.

86 bottom   A mock-up of aerodynamic flow paths on a Porsche 356 Coupe made using strands of wool glued to the vehicle's body. Aerodynamics have always played an important role at Porsche.

The 356 Porsche series, nevertheless, was soon no longer based on a mid-engine layout, but on a redesigned body with a rear-mounted engine. The first fifty cars with aluminum bodywork were handbuilt in Gmünd, Carinthia (Austria) where, in November 1944, the design studio had been transferred from its previous location in Stuttgart, all under the new company name of Porsche-Konstruktionen-G.m.b.H. Later, in 1950, the company returned to Stuttgart-Zuffenhausen. Production began again on the premises of the Reutter Bodyworks which, by the end of 1949, had already been commissioned to build 500 steel bodies. The first series production car left the Stuttgart factory on Holy Thursday April 6th, 1950. These first 356s, however, did not bear the Porsche emblem, which was not invented until 1952–1953. The word "Porsche" was all that appeared on the front hood and rear of the car.

86-87 *It wasn't long before Porsche outgrew its production facilities in Gmünd and moved to Stuttgart. It was only after this move that series production in the true sense began.*

88 *The oldest existing Porsche 356 to have been produced in Zuffenhausen. This vehicle is not in the Porsche Museum but in the beautiful Prototype Car Museum in Hamburg.*

89 *This vehicle (chassis number 5047) was shipped to Eduard Winter, a Berlin-based Volkswagen and Porsche dealer, on August 4th, 1950. It was the very first car he sold. The buyer was an American writer living in Berlin.*

The first series of the 356 was produced between 1948 and 1955 in two versions, a two-door coupe and a cabriolet, with four different engine configurations. These first models were readily distinguishable by their split-screen windshield with a central vertical bar. Models built after 1952, instead, had a one-piece center-creased, or curved windshield. The interior was equipped with a white, three-spoke steering wheel and a horn ring. The interior ignition block and switch were to the left of the steering wheel — where else, right? The fuel level had to be checked by hand with a notched wooden dipstick, inserted vertically into the tank. Standard equipment included a double, bench-style front seat for driver and passenger, with individual seats available as options.

Initially the small 1.1 liter engine produced 40 hp, soon followed by a 1300 that developed 44 hp, which, in turn, was followed by a 1500 that produced 55 hp and a 1500 S version, that developed 70. Starting in 1953 the vertical pushrod or Fuhrmann engine also became available. This, too, started out with a 1.5-liter capacity, but its four camshafts allowed the pushrod engines to attain a 100 hp rating. This engine would have been perfect for the 1952 Roadster, of which Glaser only produced 15 examples. Despite the fact that this version had to make do with 70 hp it could still reach a speed of 109 mph (175 km/h). The Speedster, an open top sports car was produced in 1954 based on the Roadster and was first intended exclusively for export to the US. It had a flat windshield and a fully foldable convertible top that was lower than that of the cabriolet. The bucket seats emphasized the model's sports character. The doors featured side curtains instead of wind-down windows.

At this point it's imperative to dedicate a few words to a man of fundamental importance to Porsche. Max Hoffmann, an Austrian who emigrated to New York at the end of World War II. Formerly a pilot, he soon began to import European cars into the United States and it was not long before this enterprise found him crossing paths with the Porsche. The first three 356s were imported in 1950. By 1951 this number had grown to thirty-two and by 1954 it had become a massive six hundred. These small 356 vehicles were as expensive as a Cadillac costing about $4,000, but it wasn't long before Hoffmann began to introduce them to the racing world and word of the Porsche's virtues spread quickly. The great Briggs Cunningham was one of America's first Porsche customers. Thus encouraged by Hoffmann, and on his advice that "The US market needs a car with a price tag lower than $3,000," Porsche also began to build the Speedster. The first Porsche James Dean bought was a Speedster, which he later substituted for a 550 Spyder, the car in which he lost his life in 1955. Porsche's reputation was in no way damaged by this incident. Quite the opposite. Even today the US remains Porsche's most important market. As it turned out, not only did Max Hoffmann play a crucial role for Porsche, but he was also the force behind the development of the famous Mercedes 300 SL, with its gullwing doors, and the fabulous BMW 507. Legend also has it that Hoffmann told Ferry Porsche that the car must have an emblem worthy of the car and that, even before the end of their conversation, Porsche had sketched a design on a table napkin. The fact that both Porsche and Ferrari have more or less the same horse in their badge is obviously a coincidence.

The 356 A Porsche was built from October 1955 to September 1959 as a Coupe, Cabriolet, and Speedster. From 1958 there was also as a Convertible D, which differed from the Speedster in that it had a slightly higher windshield, a convertible top with a larger rear window, roll-up side windows and normal, padded seats instead of bucket seats. The "D" stands for the Drauz Body Shop of Heilbronn, which supplied the convertible tops. Starting in 1957 both the Cabriolet and Speedster came with an optional hardtop.

The evolution of the 356 A was seamless throughout the years of its production, despite the fact that not a year went by without some modifications, large or small. The steering damper was improved giving the front wheels improved road contact, while two torsion bars, each consisting of eight leaves, softened the front suspensions. An additional improvement consisted of larger brake cylinders. The horsepower, too, was constantly increasing. The original 1600 produced 60 hp and could reach 99 mph (160 km/h). The 1600 S had 75 hp and could reach speeds up to 109 mph (175 km/h). Later models included the 1600 GS Carrera de Luxe, equipped with a 105 hp pushrod engine and capable of attaining a speed of 124 mph (200 km/h), the Gran Turismo, with 110 hp, and the 1959 Carrera 1600 GT with 115 hp. This last car was a true sports car, perfect even in the hands of the amateur racer, especially because its aluminum hood and bucket seats made it lighter than the other cars in the series. For racing, it was also possible to order as original equipment self-locking differential, a sports exhaust pipe system, central locking wheel nuts (also known as Rudge hubs), trumpet air intakes instead of air filters and an electrically heated windshield. The Carrera 1600 GT was instantly recognizable by its six, signature supplementary air intakes located left and right of the engine grill.

90-91 This 1956 Porsche 356 is now on display in the Porsche Museum. You can tell from the wheels with the central locking wheel nuts that this vehicle enjoyed a racing career.

91 The 356 dashboard is a clear indication of the first Porsche's origins–the Volkswagen Beetle.
The classic layout has remained essentially unchanged to date.

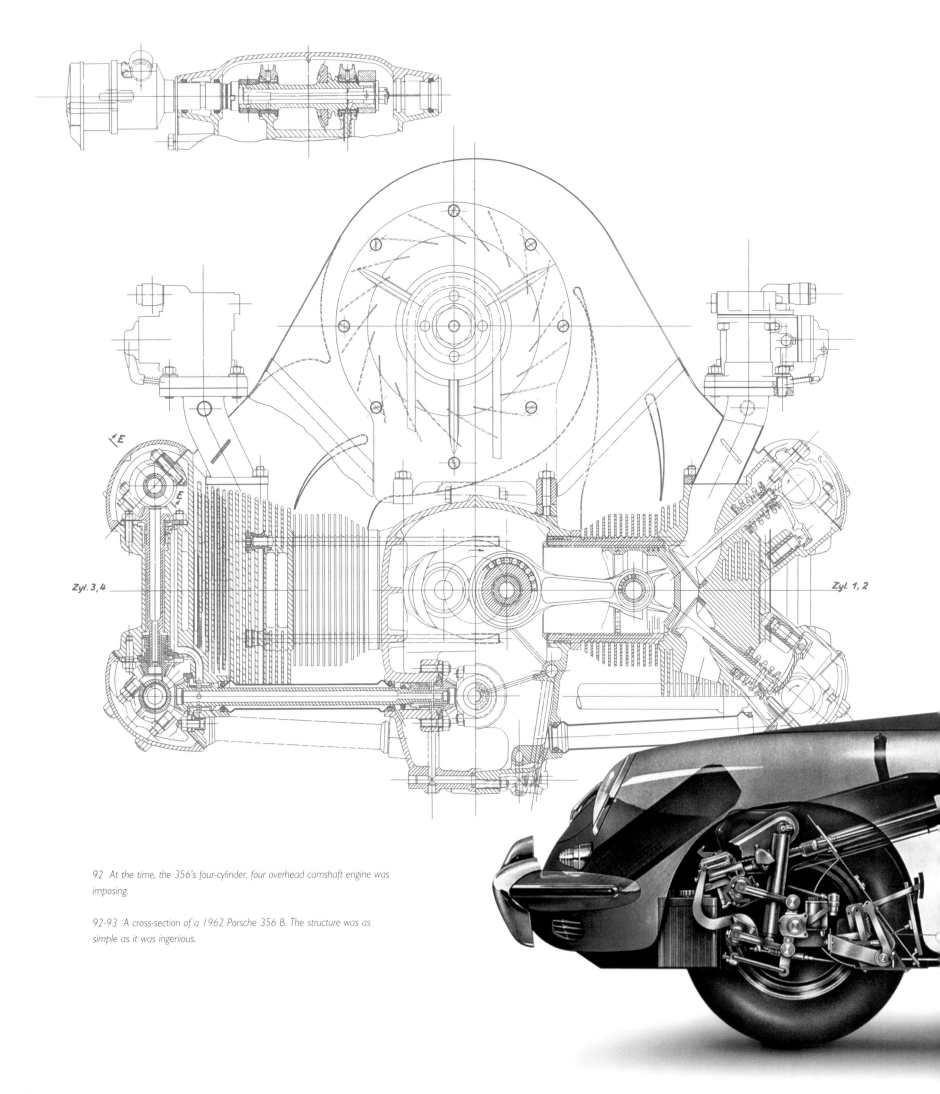

Zyl. 3, 4

Zyl. 1, 2

92 At the time, the 356's four-cylinder, four overhead camshaft engine was
imposing.

92-93 A cross-section of a 1962 Porsche 356 B. The structure was as
simple as it was ingenious.

The most striking difference between the Porsche 356 B and A models was the slightly higher mounting of the headlights and the less rounded shape of the fenders. Even the bumpers were placed higher up, which made it possible to place the air intakes for the new, light alloy disc brakes in the apron. The Porsche badge was now placed on the hub caps. The Super 90 and the Carrera had a camber compensator on the rear axle. This reduced oversteer and the tendency for the rear end to break away when cornering fast by transferring the load from the outside wheel to the less-loaded wheel on the inside of the bend thus increasing its downforce. The 356 B was built between the fall of 1959 and 1961 in all three versions Coupe, Cabriolet/Hardtop and Roadster. The Roadster was the successor to the Convertible D.

Starting in 1960, Karmann of Osnabrück produced a hardtop version with the hard top welded in place, which differed in its profile from the classic Porsche Coupe in its notched roof line (practically a notch back), and in its thin central struts and larger rear window, all of which made it look more like the Cabriolet-Hardtop. Production of the Roadster, until then produced by D'Ieteren of Brussels, ended in 1962. For the 1962 model-year the 356 B underwent further modifications. The engine hood had two ventilation grills, the front and rear hoods had a much more flattened profile, the external fuel filler pipe was placed under a flap in the right front fender and the tank was flattened to allow for more baggage space. The available configurations were 1600 with 60 hp, 1600 S with 75 hp, 1600 S-90 with 90 hp and 2000 Carrera GS with an impressive 130 hp.

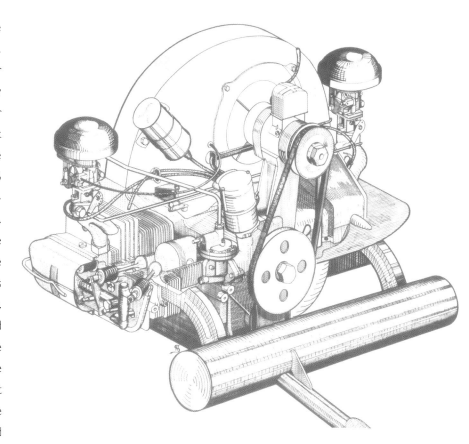

93 The first 356 engines were not much more than a powerful version of the Volkswagen Beetle's engine.

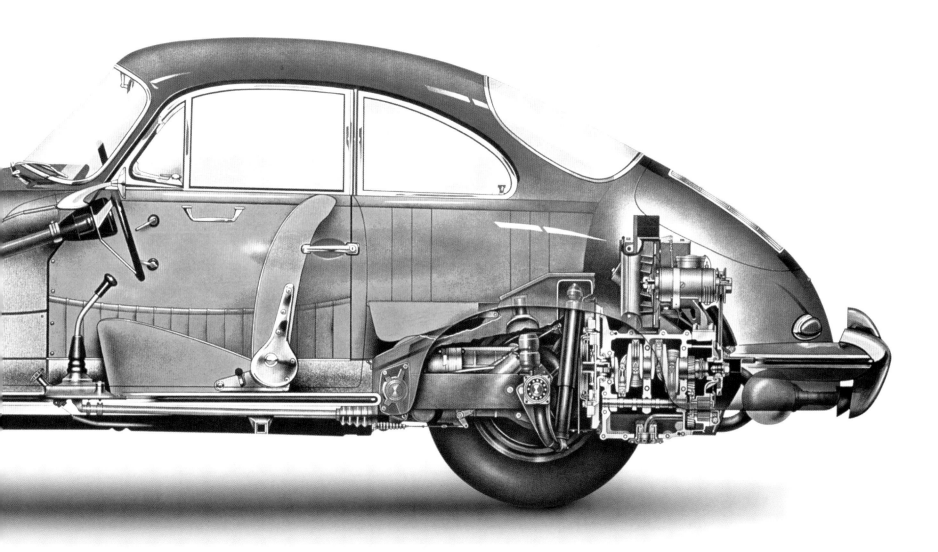

94-95 A 1959 Speedster. The first models dated back to 1954 and had originally been intended solely for export to the U.S. The windows were removable.

The 356 Carrera 2000 GS 2, available in the Coupe and Cabriolet versions, was a fabulous everyday driving car. It was also the first Porsche series car with disc brakes made in-house, also different in that the discs were gripped by the caliper from the inside edge and the outside edge was fixed to a star-shaped hub. In its standard version the Carrera could accelerate from 0 to 62 mph (0 to 100 km/h) in under nine seconds, but at 23,700 German marks (about 39,500 GBP), it was unashamedly expensive (the Cabriolet was 24,850 German marks, about 41,000 GBP). For those wanting still more, there was the sportier version, the 2000 GS-GT with light alloy doors and hoods, a wooden steering wheel, Plexiglas side windows and rear screen and no back seats or bumper overriders. Overriders were usually removed for racing. The engine's power was increased to 155 hp at 6,600 rpm and the compression ratio was elevated to 9.8:1. The GT's 29-gallon (110-liter) capacity fuel tank (other models had a 13.2 gallon/50-liter capacity tank) was combined with an external fuel filler pipe located in the front hood. At the time, the vehicle's price was 26,700 German marks (about 22,000 GBP).

For the 1962 24 Hours of Le Mans Porsche produced a prototype equipped with a "2000" engine, and body-work designed especially for high-speed circuits. The nose was lowered and the roofline was abruptly cut-off, a stark departure from the classic fluid profile of the 356 series. The resulting vehicle shape earned it the nickname *Dreikantschaber* (triangular scraper). In 1960 twenty one examples of the 356 Carrera GTL Abarth were produced featuring Abarth-designed aerodynamic body. The car's cockpit was stripped of all luxury elements, reducing the overall weight by 331 lbs (150 kg). The Abarth's equipment included dry sump lubrication, a 12V electrical system, dual ignition, four-speed gearbox with a choice of ratios and a self-locking differential. It also included a 21-gallon (80-liter) fuel tank, a sport exhaust system, special trumpet air intakes, seat belts, roll bar, and central locking wheel nuts. A 135 hp engine gave it a noteworthy speed of 146 mph (235 km/h).

96-97 top Another Speedster. This one was from 1957. With its 1.6-liter engine it could reach a top speed of almost 124 mph (200 km/h) thanks to the fact that it barely weighed 1874 lbs (850 kg).

96-97 bottom The Carrera Speedster was essentially a competition car, given that the standard version was among the fastest cars Porsche had on the market at the time. Almost all the Speedsters ended up in the States.

Lastly, the Porsche 356 C, produced from the middle of 1963 to April 1965, was almost identical externally to the 356 B. The most striking elements were the new wheel rims with simpler hub caps that no longer bore the Porsche badge. This change was a direct result of the addition of disc brakes to all the cars in the series (ATE brakes produced under a Dunlop license). The rear compensating spring was available only as an option, as was the self-locking differential.

The versions available, including the Carrera, were reduced to three. The 60 hp version (also nicknamed *Dame* or *Lady*) was done away with. The only available body styles were coupe or cabriolet. The Carrera 2 continued to be produced without modifications. For racing and rallies the 1600 CS was recommended. Race equipment included either an 18.5- or 23.7-gallon (70- or 90-liter) fuel tank, trumpet air intakes in place of air filters, a roll-bar, an underbody protection plate for engine and gearbox, Plexiglas rear window, bucket seats, light alloy 15-inch wheel rims and a rear axle compensating spring. The sump, cylinders and cylinder head were made of light alloy.

Porsche 911 — The Beginnings

It is often said that the Porsche 911 was born of necessity. By the early 1960s, the 356 was outdated and the company urgently needed to replace it with a bigger, more powerful successor. There may be some truth to this, but to fully understand the genesis of the 911 one has to go back to the mid 1950s when, despite the fact that the 356 was by no means in a state of crisis (its best years were yet to come), work began to intensify on a new model under development in Stuttgart. This was probably not so much out of necessity, as for the purpose of providing a successor for the only existing model. This may be a wild guess, but not altogether unfounded given the behind-the-scenes details that went into the development of the 911.

In the mid 1950s, then, the 356 was in great shape even though Porsche's clientele made it clear they wanted not only additional space for back-seat passengers, but also more luggage room. German engineers knew that sooner or later the 4-cylinder, air-cooled VW Beetle engine would have reached its limit in terms of the amount of power it could generate. A 1.6-liter engine had already seemed to push the limit, but the Porsche technicians did manage to produce a 2.0-liter for the Carrera model, an enormous effort that only confirmed the need to eventually come up with a six-cylinder engine. Thus began a period of research, actually already begun in the early 1950s with a 356 four-door known as Type 530 designed by Erwin Komenda, the designer of the Beetle and the Type 356. Given that the designers were already busy working day and night on other projects and having the earlier 530 to fall back on was a good stimulus.

In July 1957 a famous designer appeared on the scene. Count Albrecht von Schlitz gen. von Görtz und von Wrisberg, to give him his full name and title, was born on January 12th, 1914 in Brunkensen/Alfeld. Stories about Albrecht Görtz as he was universally known, are endless. We'll limit ourselves here to saying that, starting in 1953, he worked for BMW, where he designed the stupendous 507 and the grossly underestimated 503 (about which Pinin Farina once remarked "the 507 isn't bad, but the 503 is simply extraordinary"). Both designs earned him wide fame in Germany. Görtz worked both in Stuttgart and New York. He designed two models for Porsche. One was very Americanized ("A beautiful Görtz, but not a Porsche", was what Ferry Porsche said about it), and the other, the Type 695, which was much more Porsche-like. Nevertheless, the cooperation between Görtz and Porsche barely lasted nine months, at the conclusion of which the collaboration ended. Most books about the 911 neglect to mention the fact that Görtz worked for Porsche.

By 1959 the need to find a successor, or at least an addition to the 356 family, could no longer be put off. On August 28th Ferdinand Alexander Porsche, known as "Butzi" joined the company and began work on a car that would later turn out to be his greatest success. He was initially inspired by the Type 530, adopting its 7.9-ft (2.4-m) wheelbase (356: 6.9ft/2.1 m), and designing a car that would eventually become famous like the Type 754 T7. A first, scaled down clay model was ready by October 9th, and was so well-received in-house that during the 1959–1960 Christmas Holiday season a 1:1 scale model of it was made with the 356 axles. In retrospect, one can't help but be pleasantly surprised and amazed at how closely Butzi's first design resembled the final car.

99 *"Butzi" Porsche at work on a project that might have been one of Görtz's designs.*

As previously mentioned, the Type 747 T7 had a 7.9 ft (2.4 m) wheelbase, but Ferry Porsche insisted at all costs that it not exceed 7.2 ft (2.2 m). So, it was back to square one. F. A. Porsche returned to the drawing board to work on the Type 644 T8. Erwin Komenda reappeared on the scene with the Type 754 T9, designed in three different versions - T9/1, T9/2 and T9/3. Komenda's design, however, not only lacked elegance, but also harmony and sheer force and he soon dropped out of the competition. In 1961 Ferdinand Alexander Porsche was promoted to Manager of the Design Department, a clear indication of the direction the company was about to take.

To start out with, the Type 644 T8 had a 6.9 ft (2.1 m) wheelbase and was a two-seater. "Butzi" added 3.9 in. (100 mm), transforming it into a 2+2. By October 1961 it was felt there was no time to lose. By mid April 1962 the first mock-up model and one test model were complete. A lot of details, such as the placement of the fuel filler pipe still had to be worked out and were not definitively decided until just three weeks prior to the IAA.

During this period Karmann of Osnabrück, a longtime partner of Porsche's, began making the frame-forming equipment, given the ambitious plan to start production of the series immediately following the fall 1963 IAA. The first two models were inspected and approved by the directors of Porsche in Osnabrück on November 15th, 1962. Some question remains with regards to this time frame inasmuch as Helmuth Bott, who was in charge of development, test-drove the first prototype of the model then called the 901, on November 9th, 1962. The definitive design of the interior was still behind schedule. One design was ready by the end of March 1963 and soon after that a final version, the product of the synthesis of two studies, was chosen for the test-model III. Another interesting aspect is that the long incubation period between June 26th and December 18th, 1963 goes to show the considerable level of improvisation that went into the new model. Not only, but these designs show four different coupes (one with a folding roof and one with a removable steel top) as well as two other convertibles. No one at Porsche, however, wanted to make any final decisions about production until after the IAA, where they hoped to watch, judge, and test the reaction to the new car. In fact, no one was yet fully satisfied: "The day this car is finally finished, we can all go to the locker room for a shower" was the opinion of Ernst Bolt, manager of the model design group.

A quick note about the car's nomenclature is in order here. In correspondence dated 17th May 1962, it is first referred to as the 901, with the T8 suffix. The suggestion that "901" stood for internal project number 901 (counting from the inception of Porsche's planning department in 1937) is unfounded, since Porsche never adopted a sequential numbering system.

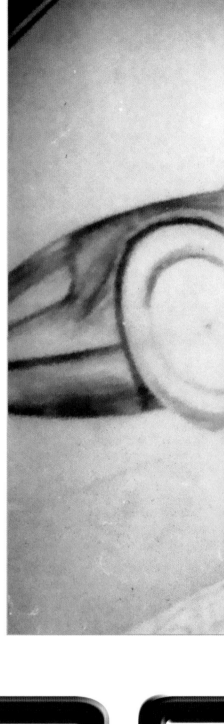

100-101 There's no doubt that it was "Butzi" Porsche who designed the lines of the 904. It's safe to assume that he designed the 901/911 too, even though some sources doubt this.

The backstage reality is altogether different and undoubtedly hints at the truth. In the early 1960s the sales networks of Volkswagen and Porsche were to have been joined. As a result, the Wolfsburg car maker reviewed the available classes of numbers for its spare parts. The 900 series numbers were the only ones available. The 901 had been intended as the first model number for the planned joint venture. This is the reason why in the past and even today the first digit of all Porsche model numbers is a 9. At that time, no one could know, of course, that things would turn out differently, not until September 12th, 1963, the opening day of the IAA.

What about the technical aspects? Thanks to the new 2-liter engine of the Carrera 2, better known as the "bevel gear engine," Porsche held an ace up its sleeve at the end of 1961. The power output of 130 hp in the series version was no small matter at the end of the early 1960s. The engine was still very complex and expensive to produce, let alone much too complicated for large-scale production. Back then, however, when the Carrera first made its market debut, there was no doubt that the 356 would have a worthy successor and that for this new model an engine would be required that was at least as powerful as the one of the car with the camshaft bevel gear. Basically, Porsche was already dealing in 8-cylinder cars, too, in those years (Types 753 and 771) for the Formula 1 single-seat er Type 804, but even these engines couldn't be produced on a large scale. Consequently, Ferry Porsche opted for a fair compromise - a six-cylinder - also with an eye to keeping development costs in check. The requirements were two: a two-liter capacity and 130 hp.

First time around with this combination, under the supervision of Klaus von Rücker, didn't go so well. The Type 745 was relatively low in height, which would have made it possible to lay it flat on the platform, but its pushrod valves were a somewhat unoriginal solution. Furthermore, it couldn't reach high engine speeds and could not top 6,500 rpm, which limited its maximum output to 120 hp.

The engine capacity was increased to 2.2 liters to make the desired 130 hp output possible, but the engine was ultimately a failure, even though later it was used in the Type 754 T7. Ferry had no desire to continue experimenting with pushrods. He preferred to direct his attention to the overhead camshaft.

At this point, three other players appeared on the scene - Hans Tomala, Hans Metzger and Ferdinand Piëch. Tomala had replaced von Rücker in 1962 and Metzger came out of the race design office to work on plans for the Type 821. While Piëch was still a student at the Polytechnic ETH of Zurich during these early planning stages of the spring of 1962, his opinions carried a lot of weight because he was a member of the Porsche family. It was soon established that the camshaft control for each head should occur by means of oil-pressure driven chains and belts. As Metzger said, "Given the fact that we have decided to have two camshafts, we might as well place them in the cylinder heads at the outset". As already mentioned, the camshaft bevel gear drive was too costly, as was the gear drive, while the toothed-belt was not yet considered reliable. Obviously, even the Type 821 had a boxer layout, even though it was widely known that in boxer engines oil becomes clogged in the external cylinder block when the car goes around a curve at high speed. To counter this problem, a significantly taller oil sump was designed, while a centrally mounted fan was envisioned for the cooling system.

The type 821 engine was transformed, without interruption, into the Type 901/01 with the new nomenclature being first used on January 9th, 1963. The main difference with respect to the Type 821 was in the lubrication system. Despite the decisively higher costs involved, Metzger and Piëch insisted on dry sump lubrication. To this end, however, a crankshaft had to be added to drive the oil pumps. The combustion chambers were also redesigned by Metzger and the valves were placed at a 59° angle from the vertical; the intake valves were angled at 27°, the exhaust valves at 32°). The individual cylinders and cylinder heads of the Formula 1 8-cylinder engines were re-adopted. From the very start, then, incremental increases in the number of cylinders had been considered. The evolution of the Type 901/01 had unfolded very rapidly, but the final result was grandiose, to say the least, as we can still affirm today. Even the figures lived up to expectations - 2 liters (1,991 cc), 131 hp at 6,100 rpm, maximum torque of 17.8 kpm at 4,300 rpm (in those days one didn't use Newton meters, today's equivalent would be 128,7 lb.-ft. or 174,6 Nm).

Clearly the running gear also needed to be updated, given that the 356 still had a welded front-end axle and a Beetle-derived rear-end axle. In fact, over the years Porsche had been eager to introduce improvements. On one 356, for instance, a Mercedes 180 front axle assembly with double arms (complete with recirculating-ball steering gear) had been used. For the new model, however, this would clearly not suffice. In 1959, immediately following approval, suspension specialists Leopold Schmid and Helmut Rompold embarked on a series of intense tests on a new model. By the start of 1961, however, progress had been slow and doubts that the new running gear would be ready by July of 1963 began to spread. In fact, it had already been established by 1961 that, given the burning desire to provide a larger luggage compartment, nothing short of a frame with MacPherson struts would do.

102 Ferry (left) and "Butzi" Porsche take a close look at the exhaust system of one of the first models of the 901/911.

103 Ferry (right) and "Butzi" Porsche examine the clay model of a 356. To the left is a 1:1 scale plasticine model of the 695 series.

104 "Butzi" Porsche with his greatest work of art, the 901/911, in 1963.

It was soon realized, however, that with the transverse arm MacPherson-type suspension, the auxiliary frame would no longer be necessary. This new solution, known as front coil-spring suspension and first introduced at the beginning of 1963, seemed so likely to be successful, that the necessary parts were immediately ordered. It all worked out remarkably well once a stabilizer bar had been added to improve performance on curves. This bar was positioned crosswise to the vehicle's longitudinal axis and connected the two front wheels by means of a series of levers and articulated joints. As far as the steering is concerned, a drive box with rack-and-pinion was used, which made it possible to mount it low down just above the platform of the frame. The steering column was jointed in two places, both because this guaranteed extra safety and because it made it possible to mount the rack-and-pinion steering in the center of the car, thereby making it easy to produce with either left- or right-hand drive versions.

At this point all that was missing was the rear axle suspension. The first prototype still had the 356 setup. It wasn't until the middle of 1962 that it was decided that, no matter what the cost, an independent suspension system would be used. Just

105 *Ferdinand Piëch, Ferdinand Alexander Porsche and Ferry Porsche together with the 901/911 development team.*

as in the 356, the back wheels were still anchored to trailing arms supported by transverse torsion bars. Telescopic shock absorbers were added behind the wheels, with ample spring extension. The first test results seemed positive but, in the months that followed, it became apparent that an overall fine-tuning would be needed, especially where the camber angle and angle of incidence were concerned. When Ferry Porsche test drove one of the pre-prototype models, however, it was only a few hours before he found fault with the inadequate steering control on the straight road. Numerous modifications were made. The axle mountings, for example, which were still adjustable on the prototypes, were welded in place. But the 0 series was already on the production line and it was too late to change them. No wonder, then, the first 911s were re-baptized "slow worms," because of their poor handling on the straight. Following the first road test, reviewed in the September 1965 issue of the German magazine "Auto, Motor und Sport," journalist Reinhard Seiffert criticized "the insufficient directional stability on uneven road surfaces, or where there is side wind," as well as the "heavy steering that's oversensitive to uneven road surfaces."

At last the big day arrived. The 901 was more or less ready as planned and shortly after 7:00 p.m. on September 10th, 1963 it was unveiled at the Porsche stand initially appearing to be overshadowed by the 356. As it was, it wasn't really ready at all. All there was in the motor compartment was a mock-up of the new six-cylinder engine. It had a dual exhaust system. There were no model tags, bumper guards, or side moldings. The car that exhibited was prototype no. 5, frame number 13325; it was produced by Karmann and was canary yellow.

The IAA wasn't as popular a show in 1963 as it is today, and the exhibition spaces weren't as spacious. However, the show with over 850,000 visitors was already one of the most important in the world and for Porsche it was a critically important appearance on home ground. No sooner was the veil lifted from the new Porsche, than a Mercedes delegation, which was also introducing a completely new model, the 230 SL, later known as the "Pagoda" and a direct competitor of the Porsche, appeared near the Porsche stand. The senior engineers of the three-pointed star quickly withdrew in some dismay. A car such as the 901 had been thought technically impossible but now there it was in all its glory, stealing the show from Mercedes-Benz.

Even before the show, Porsche had announced the car's base list price as 23,900 marks (about 197,000 GBP), which included leather upholstery (as it turned out these interiors weren't even available as an option during the launch phase). It was a risky price to set for a number of reasons, among which was the fact it was a full 7,000 marks more expensive than the 356, let alone the fact that Porsche wasn't even sure it could deliver the first cars on schedule. Potential customers were promised delivery of the 901s in the summer of 1964, but staff members themselves were skeptical about the ability to live up to that promise.

Despite the new Porsche model, there were still 400 customers who expressed interest in buying the 356, 280 of whom would welcome an opportunity to test drive it, something that even Porsche would never have anticipated until then. Of course, the first contracts for purchase of the 901 were also signed at that time, but the number was not released.

106 and 107 One of the very first 911s (1964), now exhibited in the Porsche museum. The 911s of that model-year are now very expensive, despite their less-than-impressive performance.

In all, 13 prototypes were built before the launch of the series. Those with serial numbers between 13321 and 13327, pre-production, to which two test cars for the 902 were added, with numbers 13328/13329 and four more vehicles at the end of 1964 (from 13330 to 13333). Today only one of these vehicles, no. 7, remains, in the hands of an American car collector. This car was purchased in 1965 by Richard von Frankenberg, another significant name in the history of the Porsche. It remained stored in Italy for several years until the early 1980s, when it reappeared on the scene in the US.

Like other prototypes of this series, no. 7 also had a nickname: Barbarossa. The others were Sturmvogel – Storm Bird (no. 1), Fledermaus - Bat (no. 2), Blaumeise – Blue Tit (no. 3), Zitronenfalter – Brimstone Butterfly (no. 4) and Quickblau – Quick Blue (no. 6).

At this point, it's time to explain how the car got its 911 name. In October 1964, after the Paris Auto Show, Peugeot, which held the exclusive rights to all three digit car designations with a zero in the middle vetoed the 901 nomenclature. Porsche did not dispute this claim as the law was clear on the subject. On the other hand, an immediate solution had to be found, because the first specimens of the 901 series would be ready for delivery on November 16th. The solution of choice was the least expensive: given the fact that the 901 molds were already made, all Porsche did was replace the 0 with a second 1.

Porsche 914

Maybe it really was a family affair. In the mid 1960s the principal players were Heinrich Nordhoff, then head of Volkswagen, who was desperately searching for a successor to the Karmann-Ghia models that were based on the VW Beetle, and Ferry Porsche, tasked with finding a successor to the 356 as sales of the 912 were not going according to plan. Elisabeth, Nordhoff's daughter, was married to Ferry's nephew, Ernst Piëch. It was easy to see why the two men knew each other so well, even on a personal level. It was under these circumstances that Nordhoff and Porsche agreed that Porsche would participate in the design of a Volkswagen sport model and that each company would market the car under its own brand.

A good deal for both, or so it seemed. But then, on April 12th, 1968, not long after the March 1st introduction of the first 914 prototype, Heinrich Nordhoff died. It seems his successor, Kurt Lotz, who had no ties with either the Porsche or Piëch families, did not respect the previous gentleman's agreement and held that Porsche should contribute to the material costs at a minimum. The Stuttgart leaders saw this as too burdensome, however. As a compromise, the "VW-Porsche Vertriebs GmbH" company was founded at the beginning of 1969 and was soon afterwards moved from Porsche's old stamping ground in Stuttgart, where all the design work had been carried out, to Ludwigsburg. The new model was introduced on September 11th, 1969, at the Frankfurt IAA. Initially the Volkswagen-Porsche 914/4 was equipped with the four-cylinder, 1.7-liter engine, with its modest 80 hp, also used in the Volkswagen 411E. The car was produced by Karmann of Osnabrück. The next model to follow was the 914/6, equipped with the two-liter, six-cylinder borrowed from the Stuttgart-produced Porsche 911T.

108 Today Porsche is part of Volkswagen Group, but the relationship between Porsche and Volkswagen really goes back to the end of the 1960s. The first joint venture was the Porsche 914.

108-109 In the U.S. the 914 was marketed as a Porsche and carried the Porsche marque. No surprise then that the States was its biggest market.

They shared the nickname "Volks-Porsche," or "the people's Porsche," also known as "Vo-Po," and an overall positive reception despite a somewhat negative reference to the Volkspolizei of what was then the German Democratic Republic. In North America the 914 was marketed with the Porsche name and all the accompanying badges (even if the identifying tag of the four-cylinder version identified it as a Volkswagen).

The Porsche 914/6 was a classic flop. The first model-year's sales were not so bad: 2,657 units were sold. This was followed by a drop of 432, in 1971, and by a total number of units sold of only 229 in 1972. These figures heralded the premature end of the 914/6, which, although it may have attained a speed of over 124 mph (200 km/h), cost an impressive 19,980 German marks (about 28,000 GBP). Not much different from the price of a 911T which had a somewhat superior performance. To offset the downturn in sales, starting in 1973 Volkswagen also offered a four-cylinder version with 100 hp, with the result that the two models were renamed 914 1.7 and 914 2.0. In some markets the power of the former was further reduced to 72 hp because of stricter emission standards. This was undoubtedly the least powerful model

ever marketed under the Porsche name. The 914 merited more recognition than it actually received. The fact remains that this two-seater, with its signature Targa-style hardtop, was the first-ever German mid-engine sports car and guaranteed an extraordinarily pleasant driving experience. Sales were not that bad either. Between 1969 and the end of production in the spring of 1976, a total of 118,978 units were produced, which made it the most widely sold sports car of its time.

Of course, there were a few interesting variations along the way. The first was the 914/6 R (better known as the 914/6 GT) of which 32 units were built and for which about 400 modification kits were also sold. The GT had massively widened wheel wells, an extra front-mounted oil cooler and, most interesting of all, a dual injection two-liter engine. The 916, of which a total of 11 units were produced, was even more powerful and easily recognized by its fixed, steel roof. The first three units had the six-cylinder 2.4 engine of the 911 S, whose 190 hp catapulted the more or less 1.1 short ton (1 metric ton) car from 0 to 62 mph (0 to 100 km/h) in about 7 seconds. The remaining 916 units were equipped with the 2.7-liter, 210 hp engine, whose performance was clearly even better. Topping these off was the 914/8 whose eight-cylinder 3-liter engine, based on the 908/3 sports version, produced at least 260 hp.

*110-111 With the flat six of the 911 T, the 914/6 was finally equipped with the engine it deserved.
Despite this it was a commercial flop and only 3,000 units were produced.*

When all was said and done, the 914 was more of a failure than a success. Despite this the Stuttgart team was more than pleased when, at the beginning of the 1970s, the Weissach Research Center was tasked by Volkswagen with planning the successor to the mid-engine model. We should not forget one fundamental point the "People's Porsche" had been a commercial success, even if this wasn't necessarily apparent from the outside. One tends to forget, even today, that the 120,000 units sold brought no small amount of cash into the coffers, even if it was mostly into those of the Wolfsburg company. When the work order arrived, Porsche had already taken the first few steps with project "K" (which would eventually produce the 928) and Volkswagen's idea to use as many existing Volkswagen-Audi parts as possible was favorably received. In Weissach the development of the EA 425 was proceeding at full speed, even if at that time the plan was for it to be an Audi.

The 1973 oil crisis, on top of a number of reasons relating to various in-house changes (the Scirocco had also been developed at the same time), pushed Rudolf Leiding, the then managing director of Volkswagen, to stop the project and to scrap production of the nearly-launched car, despite the 150 million German mark already invested. Porsche bought back the rights to the project from Volkswagen, thereby giving birth to a hugely successful model. Aside from the 911, no other model has sold as well as the 924 and the models subsequently derived from it. Sales topped the 325,000 mark. Moreover, it took the 911 twelve years to reach the 100,000 production target, while its younger sister, the 924, did so in under five years.

Like the Porsche 928, whose development dates to the same period, the 924 was also designed with a transaxle, a front-mounted engine and differential gearbox mounted at the height of the rear drive shaft. The two-liter inline four-cylinder engine, used for the very first time in a water-cooled Porsche with overhead camshaft and K-Jetronic fuel injection, developed 125 hp at 5,800 rpm, allowing the 2,381-lb (1,080-kg) car to accelerate from 0 to 62 mph (0 to 100 km/h) in 10.5 seconds. Thanks to its outstanding aerodynamic qualities (a drag coefficient of 0.36 and a frontal area of 18.94 ft2 or Cx × F = 0.36 × 1.76 m2 = 0.634), the 924 could attain a maximum speed of over 124 mph (200 km/h). One point worth noting was the 924's fuel consumption, which was somewhere between 2.6 and 3.2 gallons per 62 miles (10 and 12 liters per 100 km). The car's good handling could be attributed to Porsche's solid component engineering, with its wishbone rear suspension and its front suspension system with a transversal arm and MacPherson struts.

Turning to its more practical aspects, the same engine was also used not only in the Audi 100, but also in the Volkswagen LT van. The four-speed gears were Audi-sourced, as were the rear drum brakes. And the front wishbones? These were generously contributed by the VW Golf. And the McPherson front suspension? It came courtesy of the Beetle, along with the rear wishbones. Additional components came from the Audi 200 Turbo and the Volkswagen K70. The base price, on the other hand, was more than interesting: 23,240 German marks (about 29,000 GBP) (a basic 911 cost at least DM 32,000, about 40,000 GBP). On the flip side, you had to be content with tires that were not exactly sporty, 165 HR14 being the standard size.

The unmistakable style of the Porsche 924, designed by Harm Lagaay, was the result of a sloping front, grille-less nose with underlying air intake twinned with the electronically-controlled pop-up headlights, a streamlined side profile, and a huge rear window which doubled as a hatchback. By lifting this, one gained access to a baggage compartment that, for a sports car, offered a decidedly larger than usual volume: 13 cu.-ft. (370 liters). This could be increased by collapsing the rear seat backrests. It may have been for this reason that the 924 was renamed "the housewife's Porsche." Ernst Fuhrmann, who was the managing director at that time, made the comment "We finally have a model for women and young people."

Porsche 924

112-113 When the 924 S was introduced in 1986 it no longer had the two-liter engine from the Volkswagen LT van but now mounted a 2.5-liter Porsche engine. It was by far the best 924 ever.

113 When the Porsche 924 was first introduced a number of explanations were in order, especially where its publicity was concerned. Not all potential clients were aware that a Porsche might come with a front-mounted engine!

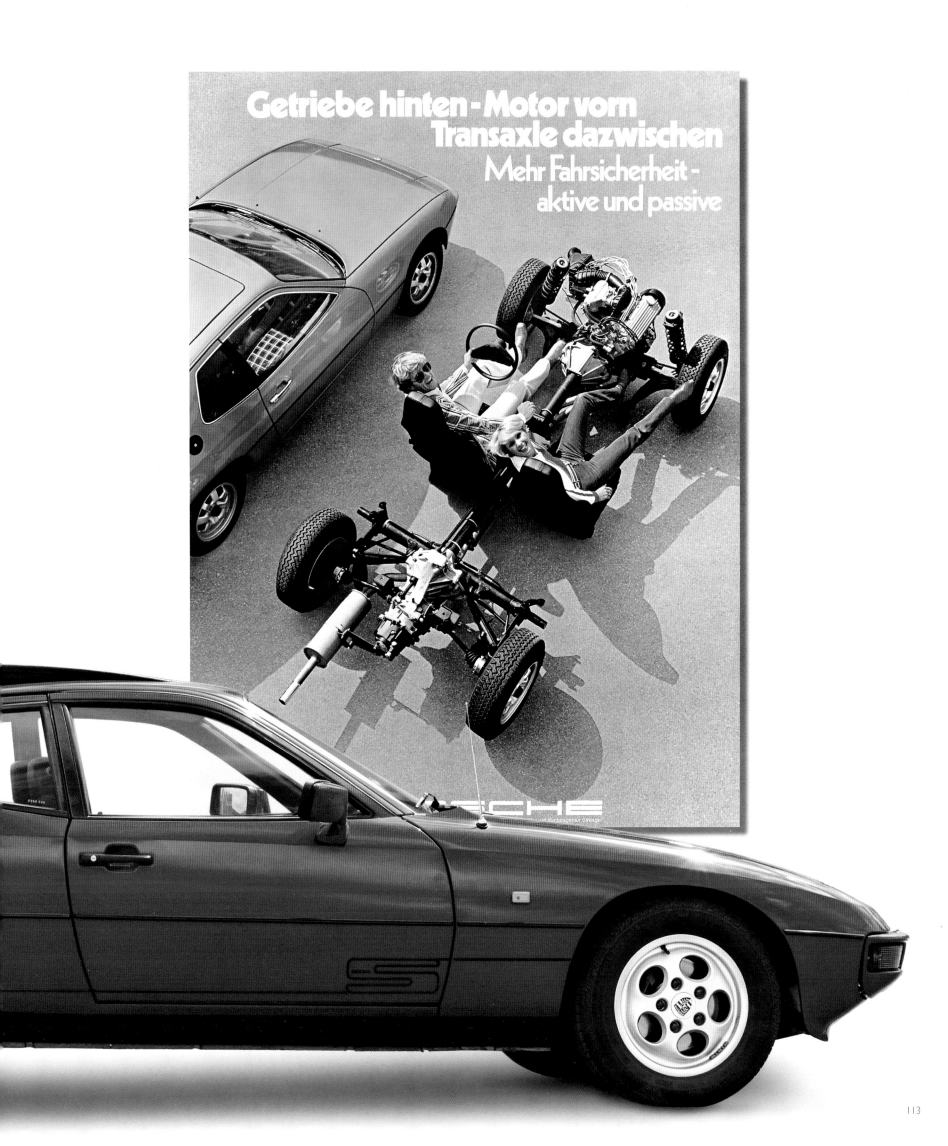

113

In November 1978 Porsche introduced yet another vehicle with an even more exciting engine and greater drivability performance: the 924 Turbo. Its turbocharged engine produced 170 hp with the same two-liter engine. It could accelerate from 0 to 62 mph (0 to 100 km/h) in just 7.8 seconds and could reach a top speed higher than its officially-certified 140 mph (225 km/h). The tires, suspension and brakes were adapted accordingly. Visually, the 924 Turbo could be distinguished from the original version by the added openings above the bumper shield, by the T-shaped air intake on the engine hood, for extra cooling, and by a less than stylish spoiler, mounted at the base of the rear window, which was later used in the base version of the 924 in the course of its evolution. Beginning with model-year 1981, the turbo engine, which dealt with the additional boost pressure by means of a bypass valve, was equipped with a fully electronic ignition system driven by this additional boost pressure. This change resulted in a 177 hp increase in engine power and, at the same time, reduced fuel consumption.

The sportier versions of this model were the 1980 924 Carrera GT, whose engine was equipped with an intercooler and could produce 210 hp. Just 400 units were produced, easily recognized by their wide wheel arches and by an air scoop mounted on the engine hood. Starting in 1981 the 924 Carrera GTS with 245 hp was also available. This was by no means the maximum performance achievable and what the engine needed now to achieve its full potential was the missing factor – development through race experience.

The Weissach engineers had already planned a first rally racecar for Barth/Kussmaul back in 1978. This was originally supposed to be equipped with a two-liter turbo engine, but never received the necessary homologation. In 1979 a car was developed for the US market. In-house it was identified as the 933, but it was better known as the 924 SCCA. It developed about 180 hp and had widened wheel wells. Sixteen

114 There's no doubt that the 924 has always been underappreciated. The transaxle layout with the front-mounted engine and differential gearbox mounted at the height of the rear drive shaft, in fact, guaranteed extraordinary handling.

115 The 924 Turbo, initially available with 170 hp, and later with 177 hp, was available starting in 1978. It served as the platform for several racecars with particularly interesting technical innovations.

units were produced and sold for the ridiculously overpriced figure of US $40,000. The 924 Carrera GTP, introduced in 1980, was developed for the 24 Hours of Le Mans. Its two-liter, turbo engine delivered 320 hp at 7,000 rpm, and weighed 2,050 lbs (930 kg). The Barth/Schurti team finished in sixth place overall. In effect, the GTP can be considered as the precursor to the 944. A year later it was the turn of the Carrera GTR, with the same two-liter engine, but as much as 375 hp at 6,500 rpm. Nineteen units were produced, sold mainly to private team drivers. The GTS was a racing version as well, destined to be sold to private customers, but with a lower performance, given that one had to be content with 245 hp, or 275 hp in the lighter, Clubsport version. A total of 59 units were produced, all in Indian Red. In 1981, Walter Rohrl was at the wheel of a GTS when he won four times in the German Championship Rally.

From the outset of the development of the light alloy V8 engine, made for the large 928, the Weissach Research Center engineers had had a second goal in mind. The possibility of cutting the V8 in half to derive an inline four cylinder that might be mounted on a future version of the 924. The result was the powerful 2.5-liter, 163 hp engine used in the 944 in 1981, whose twin balance shafts gave it smooth running and a character worthy of a six-cylinder. Beginning in 1986 this engine was used in the 924 as well, and the car was renamed the 924 S.

The new exhaust emission regulations introduced in the United States were the main reason for introducing this engine to this now-outdated model. The compression ratio was reduced. Initially its horsepower rating did not exceed 150 hp at 5,800 rpm. The suspension and braking system were borrowed from the 924, and the 5-speed gearbox was standard equipment, with the three-speed automatic transmission a not-so-appealing option. When production of the 924 S ceased, on August 1st, 1988, production of the 924 also ended. The best sales year was 1978, with 22,068 units sold, after which sales plummeted dramatically. For many years the 924 was unfairly overlooked by Porsche fans. Recently, however, used models are fetching prices that indicate an increase in the 924's value, and not only in its special editions.

Porsche 944

It is true that during its production cycle the 924 failed to enjoy the greatest reputation and it was often belittled because there wasn't a true Porsche engine under the hood. This was a problem never shared by the other not-so-well-loved 928. At the beginning of the 1980s, building on the 928 aluminum V8 engine, the Weissach engineers designed a new motor and then used it in a new series, the 944.

On the occasion of its debut in 1981, the 2.5-liter, four cylinder engine, calmed down by means of two balance counter-shafts, already produced 163 hp, allowing it to accelerate from 0 to 62 mph (0 to 100 km/h) in 8.4 seconds with the standard 5-speed gearbox or 9.6 seconds with the 3-speed automatic transmission. Esthetically speaking the 944 had nothing new to offer, given that the 924 GT and GTS had already defined the evolution of the car's design. Starting in 1986 the 944 S was available, with the same 2.5-liter engine and 190 horsepower, thanks to a new cylinder head with four valves per cylinder. In 1988 the new 944 S2 appeared, with a 211-hp three-liter which made it the largest four-cylinder engine available on the market.

116-117 Because it had an original Porsche engine under the hood, the Porsche 944 was received far more warmly by Porsche aficionados than the 924 ever was. Sales records are ample proof of this.

This happy evolution continued in 1985 with the 944 Turbo, which came with a 2.5-liter engine and an initial 220 hp. Its performance was almost equal to that of the 911 of that time and only improved as the years went by. The 250 hp 944 Turbo S attained a top speed of 162 mph (260 km/h). A cabriolet version of the 944 Turbo was also produced (528 units), as was one of the 944 S2 models (6,980 units), all made on the premises of ASC in Weinsberg.

As for sports competitions, one particularly interesting fact for the large-scale diffusion of the car was the 944 Turbo Cup Championship, held between 1986 and 1990, in which all modified models with 220 hp were qualified to participate. Roland Asch won three of these championships. During his first racing season the car still bore the 'sponsor wanted' stickers. Subsequently he was offered a proper contract and was hired as Porsche's official race driver.

Just like the 924 before it, the 944 was built in the former Audi plant, in Neckarsulm. Only the very last units of the 944 were built in Stuttgart, so the production workers could gain experience in preparation for production of the 968. In all, 163,303 units were produced. No other Porsche had been as successful as the 944.

Porsche 968

118 The engine capacity of the four-cylinder Porsche 968 was increased to three liters and for the first time the vehicle was equipped with the "VarioCam" intake valve control system. The 240 hp guaranteed excellent performance.

The 968 model, introduced in June 1991, represented both the apex and the end of the evolution of Porsche's four-cylinder sports cars. There was a great gap, both in terms of technical factors and design, between the 968 and its predecessor, the 924. Even the production sites. The 924 and 944 series were built in the Audi plant of Neckarsulm (in the case of the 944 the engines were produced in Zuffenhausen) which had the production capacity necessary. The 968, on the other hand, came out of the historic Porsche plant in Zuffenhausen. Its body work, following design elements inherited from its older sister, the 928, exuded an even greater family feeling. A smart engine evolution, including the Porsche-patented "VarioCam" intake camshaft control, allowed it to set numerous records. This three-liter engine delivered 240 hp and a maximum torque of 225 lb.-ft. (305 Nm) making it the engine with the highest torque in its class. It had a good fuel consumption and exhaust emissions were reduced by as much as 40%. ABS was standard equipment, as was the 6-speed gearbox (a four-speed automatic was also available upon request). The original version of the 968 could already reach a maximum speed of 157 mph (252 km/h) and could accelerate from 0 to 62 mph (0 to 100 km/h) in 6.5 seconds.

In 1993 Porsche introduced the 968 CS (CS stood for Clubsport), a model that was less luxurious, but had higher performance thanks to its 110-lb (50-kg) weight reduction. The 968 Turbo S, introduced in 1993, was lighter still. Each of its cylinders had two valves instead of four but, to make up for this, it had a KKK turbocompressor that could increase the engine's power to 305 hp with a maximum torque of 369 lb.-ft. (500 Nm) at 3,000 rpm. Unfortunately, Porsche asked an exorbitant price (175,000 German marks, about 106,000 GBP) for the 968 Turbo S and not surprisingly only 10 units of the series were sold. The initial plan had been to sell 100 units. The even more powerful version, the 968 Turbo RS, which was exclusively for competition, was available with either 337 or 350 hp, but was also a marketing failure. Apparently only 3 units were sold.

The demise of the large, four-cylinder engine was also due to the limited production capacity of the Zuffenhausen plant. In 1995, after 11,241 units had been produced (3,959 of these were cabriolets), the place of the 968 was taken by the Porsche Boxster.

118-119 Only 11,241 units of the Porsche 968 were produced. This is part of the reason why this particular model is so sought after by Porsche collectors. Styling played a part too. The "ugly duckling" 968 had become the "beautiful swan" 924.

The 911 Turbo made its debut in 1974, in the middle of the energy crisis. The power produced by its turbo-charged engine bordered on the incredible for those times - 260 hp at only 5,500 rpm. Rarely has the positive effect of race experience on the development of a series production car been so evident as it was on the development of this turbo engine. Porsche had already gained a lot of experience with turbocharged, twelve-cylinder engines that produced over 1,000 hp cars with its 917/10 and 917/30 models. These prototype category vehicles had dominated the 1972 and 1973 Can-Am Championship in Canada and the States.

The 911 Turbo was the first series production Porsche where extra power was obtained with an exhaust gas turbocharger. Many of the design elements of the 911 Turbo, such as the front and rear fenders, were borrowed from the famous 911 Carrera RS 3.0 and were about two inches (50 mm) wider than those of the 911 Carrera RS 2.7. This was to make room for the Fuchs light alloy wheels with low profile tires. To increase downforce on the front and rear axles and improve vehicle stability at high-speeds, the vehicle was equipped with front and rear spoilers. The large, flat rear spoiler looked like a whale's tail fin and became the distinctive feature of this sport car.

In 1977, turbo technology underwent an evolutionary advance with the addition of an air-to-air intercooler. An intercooler increases the density of the pressurized air, thereby keeping the air volume in the combustion chamber constant, while the oxygen level increases. As a result, more fuel can be injected into the combustion chamber. Thanks to this and to an increase in engine capacity to 3.3 liters, the power output of the 911 Turbo 3.3 (the car's new name) was increased to 300 hp at 5,550 rpm. Starting in 1984, customers could upgrade the standard engine's power output by 30 hp with the ''WPS'' optional, for a total of 330 hp at 5,750 rpm.

120-121 The 911 Turbo 964 series came onto the market during model year 1991. Many of its features, including the fixed rear spoiler, were adopted from the previous model (930).

121 top The engine was still the well-established Type 930 of the previous model, but now delivered 320 hp thanks to an improved engine management system and a larger intercooler.

Porsche 911 Turbo

This meant that the exhaust system had to be updated as well, with two double exhaust pipes, that ran back left and right, while an oil cooler was added mounted in the nose apron. The oil cooler could be custom ordered, either as a visible center-mounted cooler or as an auxiliary radiator hidden behind the standard front apron, but at the expense of the fog lights.

In the early eighties, it was popular in the States to modify the front end of the 930 to make it look like a racing version of the 935. So, starting in 1981, Porsche offered a flat nose version for the turbo models. The modified version was not available as an optional, but had to be ordered separately through the Special Modification Program, and was hand-made in Porsche's Repair Department. In 1987 Porsche finally heeded its customers' requests, and offered the 930 not only as a coupe, but also in targa and cabriolet versions. The standard turbo cabriolet, equipped with an automatically operated soft top was hugely successful, becoming the second most sold version after the coupe.

In 1990 the intercooler became even larger, and the power output increased to 320 hp at 5,750 rpm. On the 1993 model, Porsche introduced the Turbo 3.6 with 360 hp at 5,500 rpm coupled with the body of the 964 series. The six-cylinder boxer engine of the 911 Turbo 993 series was based on the 3.6-liter, air-cooled engine of the 911 Carrera and, thanks to its two turbochargers, developed 408 hp at 5,750 rpm.

The top of the 993 line, the 993 Turbo, made its market debut in 1995 and could be easily identified by its fixed rear spoiler. This had a twofold function. First, to increase downforce at the rear axle in order to improve high-speed stability and, second, to hide the two intercoolers that were mounted right beneath it. Since the twin turbo boxer engine already took up all the available space in the back of the vehicle, the intercoolers were placed above the engine. Unlike its 964 predecessor, the 993 Turbo was equipped with two turbo chargers and two intercoolers, which translated to even faster response and a smoother power boost. The turbo lag, typical of turbo engines, was almost eliminated and the increased power was delivered uniformly, without the obvious push during the response phase of the turbocharger. Unlike the previous model, the 993 Turbo had permanent all-wheel drive.

122-123 The turbo version of the 993 came onto the market during model year 1996. Its slightly curved fixed rear spoiler made it immediately recognisable. Its initial power output was 408 hp. Later this was upgraded to 450 hp.

For the 1998 Carrera, identified as series 996, Porsche developed a completely new engine. The only thing it shared with the previous engine was the six-cylinder boxer configuration. The main difference was that the new 3.4-liter engine, with an initial output of 300 hp (at 6,800 rpm), was water-cooled. Elimination of the cooling fan made room for a shelf behind the seats, in the place of the cabriolet version's convertible top. The switch to a water-cooled engine was made primarily to optimize cooling of the four-valve cylinders, enhance performance and to meet future gas emission standards world-wide. One interesting technical detail was the use of variable camshafts, what Porsche first called VarioCam and subsequently VarioCam Plus. At low revs the variable camshaft control made it possible to reduce gas emissions and stabilize idling. At intermediate revs, the VarioCam lowered valve lift to increase torque, while at the highest revs it assured maximum power. For the model-year 2002 this engine was significantly revised and upgraded to 3.6 liters, thanks to an increased stroke.

124-125 The Turbo version of the 996, with 420 hp, was first produced in model year 2001.
It had a 3.6-liter engine and had two intercoolers and two turbochargers.

The turbo version of the 996, with 420 hp at 6,000 rpm, was first produced in model year 2001. It had a 3.6-liter engine, two intercoolers and twin turbochargers. Unlike the Carrera, it had an external oil tank for dry-sump lubrication. The engine also featured the VarioCam Plus variable camshaft with variable valve-lift. A Tiptronic S five-speed manual gearbox was also available as an optional. Starting at the end of 2001 a power enhancement package was available as an optional on the 996 Turbo. This had previously also been available on the 993 Turbo and now on the 996 Turbo could upgrade the power output to 450 hp at 5,700 rpm and 457 lb.-ft. (620 Nm) at 3,500–4,500 rpm. Porsche achieved this upgrade by using larger turbochargers (K24 instead of K16), higher performance intercoolers, and by raising the turbo boost pressure from 0.8 bar to 0.9. They also fitted other catalyzers and exhaust pipes. At the same time, the engine control software was upgraded and the gearbox was reinforced through the use of ball bearings. The 911 Turbo S (996) model, with the same 450 hp, was available beginning in the fall of 2004.

126-127 The X59 power enhancement package, which could uprate the power output to 450 hp and had already been available for the 993, became available for the 996 at the end of 2001.

128-129 Porsche achieved this upgrade to 450 hp by using larger turbochargers (K24 instead of K16), higher performance intercoolers and by raising the turbo boost pressure (0.9 bar instead of 0.8 bar). They also revised the intake and exhaust systems. The engine control software was upgraded and the gearbox was reinforced through the use of ball bearings. The 911 Turbo S (996) model, with the same 450 hp, was available beginning in the fall of 2004.

When the new 911 Turbo series 997 made its debut in June 2006, Porsche introduced the world to something completely new. This was the first petrol-engined car to be equipped with turbochargers that had a variable turbo geometry (VTG). To resist the substantially higher exhaust gas temperatures (up to 1,000° C) compared to diesel engines, high-temperature resistant alloys had to be used. This modern turbocharger VTG for petrol engines was developed through close collaboration with BorgWarner Turbo Systems. The engine developed a maximum power of 480 hp at 6,000 rpm, and a maximum torque of 457 lb.-ft. (620 Nm) in the 1,950 to 5,000 rpm range. Maximum torque could briefly reach 502 lb.-ft. (680 Nm), thanks to the overboost function. The maximum speed was 193 mph (310 km/h). In September 2007 the 997 series was extended with the addition of the Turbo Cabrio, based on the 911 Turbo Coupe. Contrary to the general tendency to imitate the coupe-cabrio look, the third generation Turbo Cabrio also came with a three-layer soft-top, as had the earlier models that were based on the G model and the 996 series. The soft-top could be opened or closed in about 20 seconds, and was completely automatic. Like the 911 Turbo Coupe, the cabriolet version was also powered by the 3.6-liter, six-cylinder, boxer twin turbo, with two turbochargers and variable turbo geometry.

130-131 The restyled Turbo (997) was introduced in 2009. From this date onwards, this model also came with direct fuel injection and dual clutch transmission (optional). The power output was increased to 500 hp. Wheels with central locking nuts were available upon request. From 2010, the Turbo S version with 530 hp was available once again.

131 When the new 911 Turbo series 997 made its debut in June 2006, Porsche introduced the world to something completely new. This was the first petrol-engined car to be equipped with turbochargers featuring variable turbo geometry (VTG).

A restyled Turbo was introduced in 2009. From this date onwards even this model came with direct fuel injection and optional dual clutch transmission. The power output increased to 500 hp. Central locking wheel nuts were available upon request. The Turbo S version with 530 hp became available again from 2010 onwards.

On the occasion of the 2013 model-year, power output was upgraded to 520 hp for the Turbo, and 560 hp for the Turbo S. First hand experience of the performance of this all-wheel-drive car, weighing approximately 3,549 lbs (1,610 kg), is truly impressive. If you take full advantage of the boost the Turbo S guarantees, you will overwhelmed not only by the sheer power but also by the music that only a 560 hp, 553 lb.-ft. (750 Nm) twin turbo six-cylinder can produce. Another new feature was the standard active rear steering. This steers the rear wheels either in the same direction as the front wheels, or parallel to them depending on the driving speed. The Turbo also came with other new active features, always with the goal of ensuring high downforce in all driving situations. At the front end, for example, this was achieved with an inflatable, rubber spoiler that was inflated on two different levels via a compressor in the luggage compartment, thereby ensuring a much greater downforce at the front axle. The front and rear spoilers that could be set in three positions were also new features not previously available on the 997 Turbo series.

Porsche 911
The Evolution

Production of the 911 began in September 1964 (model year 1965). The the original base list price was 21,900 German marks (equivalent to about 35,000 GBP today). The new engine developed 130 hp at 6,100 rpm; two Solex carburetors produced the air-fuel mixture and optimal lubrication and internal engine cooling were ensured by dry sump lubrication. The oil cooler was located close to the engine; later versions came with an additional oil cooler in the front passenger-side bumper. The large, axial vent for cooling air was a dominant feature of the engine compartment. In addition to the first 13 prototypes of the 901, 230 units of the Type 911 were produced in the first model year, 1965 (beginning in September 1964). The 911 name/designation was not introduced until November 1964.

In 1965 demand for a more affordable Porsche led to development of the Type 912. Its 4-cylinder, 90 hp engine came straight from the 356. The rest of its equipment was more spartan in comparison with the 911. The base list price was 16,250 German marks (about 26,000 GBP). In 1965 Herbert Linge and Peter Falk, two Porsche employees, drove the 911 in its first ever automobile race, the Monte Carlo Rally, and came in fifth.

134-135 One of the very first 911s. The most legendary of all the Porsche models went into production in September 1964. That year only 230 units were produced.

At the beginning of September 1965 Porsche introduced the Targa, a new body style with a fixed roll-bar, removable top and foldable PVC rear window at the Frankfurt IAA. They introduced it with the following words, "The 911 Targa is neither a cabriolet, nor a coupe, neither a hard-top, nor a sedan, but something completely unprecedented." In fact the Targa was a direct response to repeated requests from American dealerships for a convertible version of the 911 following the great US success of the preceding model, the 356, in its cabriolet version. In the US, the safety standards for convertible cars had become so strict that many automobile manufacturers had been forced to drop convertibles from their lineups. Porsche's take on this problem was to adopt the 'necessity is the mother of invention' approach. Even so, initial response to their "invention" might be better characterized as puzzled, rather than enthusiastic. Porsche had wanted/intended to present their new design to the press as a stroke of genius, but in fact it was received/viewed as a compromise that came at the expense of aesthetics, a solution that was 'neither here nor there'. Porsche marketed the wide, stainless steel-clad roll-bar behind the car's seats, as a protective shield ("Schutzchild" in German).

136-137 The Targa enjoyed great success, especially in the States, where many clients chose to order the optional rear spoiler.

137 Porsche started production of the 911 Targa in December 1966. Shown here is "Butzi" Porsche, designer of the 911, with one of the first Targa models.

On September 21st, 1966 the 100,000th Porsche was delivered: a 912 intended as a police car. The six-cylinder, two-liter received its first power upgrade: the 911 S developed 160 hp at 7,200 rpm and reached a top speed of 140 mph (225 km/h). The suspension, too, was improved, with the addition of front and rear stabilizer bars, and new forged alloy wheels designed by the Porsche Style Center and produced by Fuchs. Even today the so-called Fuchs wheels remain famous and are considered the most distinctive of all Porsche wheels. In the racing version the two-liter engine developed as much as 210 hp; this engine was also used in the 904 and Carrera 6 (906) models.

In 1968, the 911 T made its debut with a list price of 20,000 Marks (about 29,600 GBP) and soon afterwards replaced the 912. Its six-cylinder developed 110 hp and was paired with a four-speed gearbox. The stabilizer bars had been dropped.

138-139 A great number of special sports editions and racing versions were derived from the 911. Shown here is a 2.5-liter, 250 hp ST.

This was the first car to offer the Sportomatic, a semi-automatic, four-speed transmission with a hydraulic torque converter and a clutch that disengaged automatically when the driver touched the gear stick. This unusual transmission was used until 1980. In addition to the 911 T, the 911 L, which developed 130 hp and was otherwise equipped similarly to the 911 S, was also added to the 911 family.

In 1968 the wheelbase of all the 911s was increased from 87 to 89.3 in. (2,211 to 2,268 mm): this was an effective improvement, because the early 911s were particularly unstable at high speeds. Today, the "short" 911s are in particular demand. Another change that occurred in 1968 was the addition of Bosch mechanical fuel injection: on the 911 E this translated to a power increase to 140 hp, and on the S to 170 hp. Finally, the Targa got a fixed glass rear-window.

140 The 911 E base model gives you more for your money if you're in the market for an older 911, and it's especially sought after for its classic lines.

140-141 In model-year 1969, the 140-hp 911 E replaced the 911 L. Starting in model year 1970, the engine capacity was upgraded to 2.2 liters.

In 1969 Ferdinand Piëch was named Director of Development and, at the beginning of the model year 1970, production of the 912 was terminated. For the new model year, the engine capacity was increased to 2,195 cc (with an 84 mm bore). The power of the T, E and S models was upgraded to 125, 155 and 180 hp, respectively. Starting with this model year the crankcase was cast in aluminum alloy, a change that made it decidedly more rigid. The car was also put on a slimming diet whereby the weight of the 911 S was reduced to 1,020 kg. In 1971 the engine capacity was increased again, this time to 2,341 cc (with a 70.4 mm bore). The crankshaft had counterweights for each cylinder. Power output for the three models, T, E and S increased slightly to 130, 165 and 190 hp, respectively, while maximum torque increased by 10%. One special feature was that all the engines ran on regular grade gasoline. The increasingly strict exhaust emission control regulations were beginning to make themselves felt, and in some of the export markets high-octane fuel with elevated lead levels was no longer available. The engine oil filler cap was moved to the height of the rear passenger fender, and the 911 E and 911 S gained a small, front spoiler. A new generation gearbox was also introduced at this time.

By 1972 all the 911s were equipped with front spoilers and the E and S models came with an 85-liter fuel tank. The first vehicles with K-Jetronic fuel injection were made for the US market and the wheelbase was extended to 89.4 in. (2,271 mm).

Now, let's look at the Carrera 2.7 S. In the early '70s Porsche was in dire need of a grand touring vehicle so that it might participate in the highest level competitions of even the most popular categories. Participation in the GT category required production of a minimum of 500 GT vehicles. This led to development of a model that would go on to become a legend, the 911 Carrera RS 2.7. The engine displacement was 2.7 liters (2,687 cc), thanks to an increase in bore size from 84 to 90 mm. The new cylinders were coated with Nikasil. The vehicle's maximum power was 210 hp at 6,300 rpm, and maximum torque was 188 lb.-ft. (255 Nm) at 5,100 rpm. The Carrera RS weighed 960 kg and reached a top speed of 149 mph (240 km/h), which made it the fastest German street-legal car of its time.

The price for the new sports car was only 33,000 German marks (about 43,600 GBP). The first production run was already sold out by November 1972. A second batch was planned immediately, bringing the total number of units produced to 1,036.

The most distinctive feature of the fastest 911s of that time was by any measure the fiberglass rear spoiler, famously nicknamed the "birzel" or duck tail. The Carrera was available in three versions - Sport, Touring and Racing. The suspension system had Bilstein shock absorbers and 0.6 in. (15-mm) stabilizer bars. The result of this setup was an extra rigid suspension or, to paraphrase Porsche, a very sporty suspension. With the Carrera RS it was possible to reach speeds on curves that, up to that point, had simply been unattainable for any other road-going Porsche. The official body color was "Grand Prix Weiss" (Grand Prix White), but all the standard colors and Porsche optionals were also available. The aluminum wheels (6Jx15, on the front, and 7Jx15, on the back) were available in red, blue, or green.

In 1973 (model year 1974) the G model or, more precisely, the G series made its debut. In this form, the 911 remained in production for another 16 years, until mid-1989 with the end of the K series. If one were to nitpick, only the model-year 1974 vehicles should be classified as "model G" but all the 911 models made between 1973 and 1989 are commonly referred to as "model G." The new generation, the 964, started at the same time as Model K was introduced in mid-1988.

142 With the unveiling of the Carrera RS in 1972, Porsche introduced the auto industry to one of its greatest legends. Its 2.7-liter engine developed 210 hp.

143 The 'ducktail' rear end gave the Carrera RS its distinctive look. Weighing only 2,200 lbs (1,100 kg) the vehicle could reach a top speed of 152 mph (245km/h).

Changes were significant, even when it came to the car's looks. Bumpers compliant with US safety standards were required. These were made of aluminum and were adorned with an accordion trim both in front and back that lent the 911 a distinctive look. Even the cockpit underwent significant revamping. The engine capacity was upgraded to 2.7 liters on all models and engine configurations. The basic model consisted of the 150-hp 911, followed by the 911 S with 175 hp, and the Carrera with 210 hp. Unlike the Carrera RS 2.7, however, the new top-of-the-line model did not have a rear spoiler but nevertheless could hurtle to 149 mph (240 km/h) effortlessly. The new 911s were characterized not only by their extraordinary drivability, but also by their markedly higher quality. The Carrera RS was modified for competition and, as the Carrera RSR, won the 24 Hours of Daytona and the 12 Hours of Sebring. An RSR with noticeably widened bumpers was entered in the Prototype category of the last Targa Florio and went on to win.

Following the major updates of 1973, the 1975 model-year 911 remained essentially unchanged. The only changes were to the level of comfort and to the gearbox of the 911 S. In 1975 Porsche introduced the 911 Turbo, the first production sports car to be supercharged by means of an exhaust gas turbocharger. It developed 260 hp. There were no major styling changes to the vehicle in the 1976 model-year either, but the range of available engine sizes was reduced and included the 2.7-liter 911 with 165 hp, the 200-hp Carrera with the three-liter engine and, finally, the 911 Turbo (930). The 1976 911 came with standard, four-speed transmission, but 5-speed gearbox was also available as an optional. The notorious 4-speed Sportomatic was replaced with a 3-speed Sportomatic.

Following research into development of long-life vehicles, Porsche became the first vehicle manufacturer to use flame-sprayed, zinc-galvanized steel as a standard feature on its cars, guaranteeing the vehicles against corrosion for six years. In 1985 the anti-corrosion guarantee was extended to ten years.

June 3rd, 1977 saw production of a 911 S 2.7, the 250,000th vehicle Porsche had produced since it first began making cars in 1948. Among other reasons, it was worth noting for its excellent fuel-consumption. The Bosch K-Jetronic fuel injection reduced fuel consumption of the 911 SC (3.0-liter with 180 hp) by 17% compared to the previous model. This 911 SC, the only 911 model available between 1978 and 1983 was a sort of catch-all Porsche, as it replaced both previous versions of the 911 and the Carrera. Starting in 1978, the 911 Turbo, whose engine capacity was upgraded to 3.3 liters, developed 300 hp.

Following customer complaints, the power output of the 911 SC was slightly increased from 180 to 188 hp during the 1979 model year, but performance remained the same. The vehicle still accelerated from 0 to 62 mph (0 to 100 km/h) in 7 seconds and its top speed was 140 mph (225 km/h). Available versions still consisted of the Coupe and the Targa. A more powerful version, the 911 "Moby Dick" was introduced in 1978. Its 3.2-liter, turbocharged six-cylinder, equipped with four overhead camshafts, developed 845 hp. In 1979 the version of the 911 sold in the US was the first high performance sports car to come with a regulation catalytic converter. In 1980 the power output of the 911 SC was further increased to 204 hp yet its fuel consumption still remained exemplary. 10.4 liters were all that were needed to complete a standard fuel consumption testing cycle. Other vehicles in this class paled by comparison in fuel consumption efficiency. In order to achieve such efficiency, Porsche had to significantly increase the compression ratio from 8.6:1 to 9.8:1, which also meant the 911 SC had to run on super grade gasoline. The 200,000th 911 was delivered on September 4th, 1981. This was followed by another anniversary on September 18th when the Porsche no. 300,000 was produced.

In 1982 the 911 was offered in a Cabriolet version for the first time: this was the first Porsche Cabriolet to be offered in 17 years. The previous one, the 356 Cabriolet, had left the Porsche plant in April 1965. Its basic body, obviously, was that of the 911 SC. What was known as three-bow design made it possible for the open-topped version to be 15 kg lighter than the Targa. A giant rear spoiler was also available upon request, and for those who wanted an even sportier look the "Turbo-look" package was available with the Turbo suspension.

In September 1983 the new 911 Carrera was unveiled at the Frankfurt IAA. Its engine capacity had been increased to 3.2 liters and it developed 231 hp. From the outside, the car was easily recognizable not only from the lettering of the Porsche name, but also for the fog lights, which were integrated into the front bumper shield and for its new alloy wheels.

Also unveiled at the 1983 Frankfurt IAA was the "Group B" design study, the forerunner of the Porsche 959. The "Carrera" name was added to the 911 designation. Thanks to the addition of Bosch Motronic fuel injection, power output of the 3.2-liter engine was upgraded to 231 hp. The 911 SC "4x4" won the Paris-Dakar Rally.

144 Over the years there was a steady increase in the vehicle's engine capacity. In 1973 it reached 2.7 liters in its top end model, the Carrera 2.7.

In 1983 the clutch was modified slightly to accommodate the new five-speed transmission and the canvas top of the Cabriolet was automated, so that it could be activated automatically and opened or closed in 20 seconds. On the 911 that came with a catalytic converter, power output was increased from 207 to 217 hp. Also that year, Porsche unveiled the 959, the most powerful production model available to date. This vehicle came with automatic all-wheel drive and two-stage, twin-turbo superchargers. Porsche introduced the catalytic converter technology to its German market cars in 1985. In 1986 the "Paris-Dakar" 959 won the Paris-Dakar Rally, covering a distance of 8,575 (13,800 km), the most difficult event to date.

To celebrate production of its 250,000th unit of the 911, in 1987 Porsche unveiled a commemorative edition model limited to 875 units. The 959, a sort of "super 911" equipped with cutting-edge technical solutions was presented, instead, as a street-version of a high-performance sports car. A total of 292 units of this vehicle were produced; the list price was 420,000 Marks (about 298,000 GBP). Lastly, the 911 Speedster was also unveiled at the 1987 IAA, a special series of which 2,100 units were produced. The website www.radical-classics.com describes it as follows:

The front is simply fantastic and is reminiscent of the 356 Speedster, produced between 1955 and 1958, from which it inherits the flat windshield. Its profile reminds one a little of the Italian *barchetta* of the early 1950s. Too bad then for those two humps behind the seats that look like two backpacks that just didn't manage to slip in to the vehicle's overall harmonious look. The heavy look of the tail is reinforced by the large rear end which has to house the 245/45 ZR16 tires; at the front axle, the tires are narrower, being 215/55 ZR16s. In this manner, it foreshadowed the look of the tail of the successive 911 Turbos all the way to today's. Notwithstanding, every one of the 2,102 units of the 1989 Porsche 911 Speedster were quickly sold to as many Porsche enthusiasts, thereby allowing this vehicle to join a class of supersports vehicles sure to make a good impression along the avenues of any city in the world. To show it off at its best, all this vehicle needs is two things: sunshine and lots of open space. And, in this respect, it's not surprising that the Speedster should have been designed especially with export to the US in mind. Good weather is a must for taking this car out of the garage. It should be no surprise, then, that the folding roof should be officially designated an 'emergency sunroof' and should limit visibility considerably. With the two headrests and the two headrest fairings it was practically impossible to see anything when reversing. When the sunroof was closed, parallel parking could only be achieved if you had a sixth sense of three-dimensional geometry. On the other hand, such a talent was rarely called for in Florida. Porsche was obviously aware of this shortcoming and outwardly admitted to it: "The cabrio is a closed vehicle that can also be driven as an open car." it said, "A speedster is an open car, that can also be driven with the top closed".

45 *The distinctive features of the 1973 Carrera 2.7 included black door handles and window surrounds.*

Porsche 928

A water-cooled, front-mounted V-8 engine, rear-mounted gearbox, large-dimension body and an ultra-modern design. When it made its debut in 1977, the 928 departed from all the norms and traditions that Porsche and its large array of enthusiasts had nurtured over time. The 914 and the 924 (the latter introduced in 1975) had not necessarily had to conform to these, because they were in a class that was a notch beneath them anyway. The 928, on the other hand, had been conceived as an flagship of equal standing, if not superior to the 911. When it was previewed at the Geneva Salon in 1977, it was immediately labeled a competitor, at least by hardened Porsche fans.

The aim was to design a car that would command attention not only on the merits of its technical features (front-mounted engine with transaxle and rear-mounted gearbox to optimize the weight distribution), but also for its design. The front end had a smooth and flowing low hood line that ended in an imposing tail, not to mention pop-up headlights and invisible, polyurethane bumpers. Purists deemed it too big, too heavy and not sufficiently agile. The design director, Anatole Lapine, and Wolfgang Mobius, who played a significant role in the design of its body outline, were faithful to the principle of a timeless design, to which they felt bound, rather than to passing trends. At the 1977 Geneva Salon presentation of the vehicle, Lapine stated, "Conventional vehicles become boring very quickly. The 928, instead, will last for years." This isn't at all surprising if you look at the car. And if you take into consideration the fact that the exterior appearance remained unchanged until the end of production in 1995 and that 61,000 units were sold. One certainly cannot find fault with Lapine's forecast.

146-147 For model-year 1980, a more powerful version, the 928 S, joined the 928 originally introduced at the Frankfurt IAA in September 1979. The 928 S was equipped with a more powerful engine that developed 300 hp, thanks to the higher engine capacity (4,664 cc) and a higher compression ratio.

The oil crisis, along with other factors, played a role in the 928's history at least twice. The first time, it interrupted development of the car bringing it to a halt for a full six years. The design study for a sports car designated "K" was initiated in the winter of 1971–1972 (Dr. Ernst Fuhrmann gave the go-ahead on October 21st, 1971). Shortly after the project had taken off, a stroke of luck arrived in the form of a commission by Volkswagen to produce the successor to the Volkswagen-Porsche 914, identified as project number EA 425. The main objective was to use as many Volkswagen-Audi parts as possible. This meant that Porsche could work on two similar cars at the same time. The development of the new Volkswagen-Porsche proceeded at full speed and was made a number one priority. As an external commission with high profit margins it obviously sidetracked the internal project "K." This is why project EA 425 was completed before its "elder sister." Later, when the EA 425 project was in its most advanced stages, Volkswagen abandoned it altogether and Porsche wasted no time in securing the project for itself. In 1975 the car made its debut as a Porsche 924.

The 1973 oil crisis had almost brought an end to the stalled project "K." Then, on November 15th, 1974, the Board of Directors decided to start it up again. The plan of action was made very clear. The new Porsche was not to replace the 911, but to upgrade it.

Its destiny, however, was linked to many unknowns, like Middle East oil prices and the numerous standards relating to emissions, noise, and safety. On an economic level, the effect of these factors was such that the 928 was initially supposed to run on low-octane, regular fuel. The engine was 4.5 liter rather than 5.0 liter. Nevertheless, in 1978 the 928 was named "Car-of-the-Year" by a jury of auto-industry journalists, and sales were successful from the start, contrary to expectations and despite a long waiting period for delivery. It came as no surprise, in fact, that the type of buyer the 928 attracted was different from the one that bought the 911. These buyers expected their sports cars to make a statement about their own image, but they also wanted a car that provided ease in shifting gears and ample room. The 928 was more than capable of delivering on these requirements, certainly more so than the 911. Not surprisingly, it turned out that many Mercedes customers switched to the Porsche 928.

The weight distribution was optimal, while the newly designed rear axle (known as the "Weissach axle") and, most of all, the transaxle (already introduced in the 924) reduced the tendency to oversteer in situations where the driver lifted his foot from the accelerator pedal during cornering (something inexperienced drivers, in particular, tend to do). Despite its dimensions and weight, then, its handling was relatively agile and sporty. However, critics argued that the sound of the big Porsche, with its aluminum V8 engine was not up to standard and that its performance was less than remarkable. One couldn't really argue with them. Objectively speaking, the six-cylinder "roar" and the "kick-in the-butt" were inexcusably missing. The first version of the 928 developed only 240 hp, although it was almost as fast as a 911 of that time. Only the Turbo could make its larger elder sister bite the dust. The gearbox was a 5-speed manual, or a 3-speed automatic which, by the way, were also used on the Mercedes SL and SLC.

In August 1979 the 928 S was introduced, with an increased engine size (4.6 liter/4,664 cc), greater power (300 hp), and improved performance. The 928 could accelerate from 0 to 62 mph (0 to 100 km/h) in 6.8 seconds (the same as the 911 SC of its time) and could reach a top speed of 143 mph (230 km/h). The 911 SC could attain a top speed of 146 mph (235 km/h). It took the 928 S 0.2 seconds less to accelerate from 0 to 62 mph (0 to 100 km/h), and it could reach 155 mph (250 km/h). These figures may not seem that impressive on paper, but the effect on an emotional level was right on the mark. A 155 mph (250 km/h) speed at that time was significant because, as rightly expressed in the automotive industry press, "Now the performance is as exaggeratedly high as that of the fastest cars in the world."

The right hand cylinder head of the aluminum V8 engine served as the single bank of the engine for the Porsche 944, while the S4 motors were transformed into 750-hp boat engines. The tire pressure control system was the first ever offered as a standard feature on any car worldwide (August 1988). Also worthy of note was the electronically controlled self-locking differential (March 1989). The four-seat 928 S version, with its wheelbase extended by 9.8 in. (250 mm), was given as a gift to the company President, Ferry Porsche, on the occasion of his 75th birthday.

148 The most distinctive features of the 928 S were the newly designed light alloy wheels, the small front and rear spoilers designed to improve aerodynamic flow, and the automatic, external, passenger side rear-view mirror.

149 The 928 S was available either with five-speed standard transmission or with the new four-speed automatic transmission. The automatic transmission version could accelerate as fast as the standard version. The ABS, available for the first time as an option on a Porsche, provided a smart braking system.

Those in the know, nevertheless, still found something to complain about in the 928, such as the differences between it and the 911 Turbo, whose phenomenal output never found an equal, not even in the S. Two years later, production of the original 928 was discontinued, while the evolution of the S continued. In 1983 the engine was equipped with the electronic Bosch LH-Jetronic fuel injection, with a resulting increase in power output to 310 hp. A year later one could order ABS. In 1985 the S4 came out, with four valves per cylinder and a catalytic converter. Changes that followed were made to augment the car's luxury feel, which further widened the gap between it and the 911, and definitively confirmed its calling as a grand tourer.

At the same time, an increase in engine power was in the works. In 1989 the GT made its debut with 330 hp and was followed two years later by the last evolution, the GTS, with a 5.4-liter (5,397 cc) engine and 350 hp, which enabled it to attain a speed of 171 mph (275 km/h) and accelerate from 0 to 62 mph (0 to 100 km/h) in 5.7 seconds. Even more importantly, it could brake to zero in 2.8 seconds, without the help of a racetrack barrier wall! As far as its performance was concerned, the GTS was light years ahead of the first generation of 928s while the only visual differences were limited to the wide wheel arches, the rear spoiler and the rear lights that were connected by a lighted strip. The 928 is in some quarters still little appreciated today but, fortunately, only by those who either don't really know it or know it only superficially. Market analyses, by contrast, show the greatest level of loyalty of all Porsche models to Lapine's masterpiece. Once you have driven a 928 nothing else will do. Jacky Ickx, the former Formula 1 racer considered it the best GT of its time.

150-151 *The 4.5-liter V8 engine, with a 90° bank angle, initially developed 240 hp, and was a completely original design. The cylinder block and cylinder heads were made of light alloy, and the two overhead camshafts (one per cylinder bank) were driven by a sprocket chain. The combustion chambers were wedge-shaped.*

Porsche 959

The 1980s were not Porsche's best years. Cars like the 924 and 928 had not contributed to the advancement of the brand, while sales of the immortal 911 no longer lived up to the expectations of the Stuttgart team. At the time, Peter Schutz sat at the controls of the company. When the then technical director, the engineer Helmuth Bott, proposed some modifications to the 911, Schutz listened to him with an open mind, especially because these changes would have transformed the 911 into a Group B rally car.

The most interesting modification Bott proposed regarded an innovative all-wheel drive. While he was given the go-ahead only in 1982, by the fall of 1983 the first prototype of the 959 had already been shown at the Frankfurt IAA. Public reaction, especially that of potential buyers, was enthusiastic, despite the fact that the 959 looked like a swollen, oversized 911. The entire back end of the car had been transformed into one giant spoiler. As far as the enlarged bumpers were concerned, including the Kevlar tail, Porsche had reached beyond its traditional boundaries. The car looked like an experiment on the deformation of plastics gone seriously wrong.

The hints that Porsche allowed to leak out about what was under the prototype's hood, on the other hand, stirred the appetites of more than just Porsche enthusiasts. Hidden from view was a six-cylinder boxer engine with a 2.85 liter capacity combined with twin turbochargers, all-wheel drive, and ride height variable with speed. Before the gates of the IAA had closed the 200 units required for Group B homologation had already been pre-ordered.

Before Porsche had finished putting the finishing touches to the 959 design, company engineers first focused on the racing car, officially known as the 911 4x4, but known in-house as the 953. The 953 was developed specifically to compete in the Paris–Dakar Rally, as a joint venture with the British team Prodrive, with the unexpected result that René Matge, the driver, was the first to cross the finish line. In 1985 Porsche decided to participate again, with every intention of repeating the earlier success. However, the 600 hp twin-turbo engines that had been expected for the cars were not ready and the vehicles, now officially known as the 959, were sadly withdrawn from the Rally. By contrast, in 1986 Porsche once again won two firsts in the legendary desert rally, but this success arrived too late, because the Group B class was dropped following the fatal crash of the Henry Toivonen/Sergio Cresto vehicle in the Corsica Rally. Thus the 959 racing career was abruptly interrupted.

152 Among the supercars of the '80s, the Porsche 959 was by far the most technically advanced. There was no mistaking the fact that its look was based on the legendary 911.

Finally, in 1987, things took a turn for the better, when the 959s were finally ready for delivery to customers. Not only was the car the fastest production model of its time, but it also stood as a standard-bearer for the highest technological levels. The use of Kevlar for the vehicle's bodywork has already been mentioned; to this were added polyurethane front and rear spoilers. Even the magnesium wheels were an innovation. To a some extent, the use of these made it possible to conceal the somewhat problematic tire pressure monitoring system, first introduced on the Porsche 936 at Le Mans, but which caused some problems in the 959. This model should have come with Dunlop's new Denlocs, but at the last minute Porsche decided to use Bridgestone tires.

The use of all-wheel drive was far ahead of its time, clearly an innovation considering that this was only the end of the 1980s. The rear wheels were driven through a traditional differential, while the front differential was connected to a six-speed gearbox at the main axle. In slippery conditions, the multi-plate clutch would optimize torque distribution, while the sensors detected tire traction, degree of slippage, engine speed, and the steering angle. What no computer was able to calculate, however, was the enormous power transmitted to the wheels by the twin-turbo, six-cylinder aluminum alloy engine which, in keeping with Porsche tradition, was air-cooled. The cylinder heads, on the other hand, had their own water-cooling system.

154-155 Among the new technological features introduced with the 959, were
innovative all-wheel drive and the use of materials such as Kevlar for the bodywork.

Two overhead camshafts for each cylinder bank and four valves per cylinder were a must, as was dry-sump lubrication (oil volume was an impressive 4.8 gallons/18 liters!). New sodium-filled exhaust valves were used to improve heat transfer. All of this was in addition to the already-mentioned two-stage supercharging, with two water-cooled, sequential KKK turbochargers, and the addition of two intercoolers.

The result was 450 hp and a maximum torque of 369 lb.-ft. (500 Nm) at 5,000 rpm. The 959 accelerated from 0 to 62 mph (0 to 100 km/h) in less than 4 seconds and attained a top speed of almost 199 mph (320 km/h).

There is disagreement over the exact number of Porsche 959s produced, but two figures are consistently cited: 288 and 337. The latter may very well be the most credible, especially because of the large number of test-vehicles made. In 1992, four years after the end of production, Porsche decided to launch a second series based on available spare parts and improved in several respects, especially in details relating to the unreliable variable ride height. The first units had already cost a hefty 420,000 German marks (about 268,000 GBP), but for these last eight units Porsche pulled out all the stops and asked the unthinkable price of 745,500 marks (about 476,000 GBP).

In 1988, on the occasion of its 25th anniversary, Porsche introduced the 911 Carrera 4, known in-house as Type 964. Eighty-five percent of its components were brand new in design. After 15 years in production, the 911 range sorely needed a redesign. Porsche was going through a period of crisis toward the end of the 1980s. Even the 944, a favorite which accounted for much of company turnover during those years, was no longer meeting its sales forecasts. Furthermore, the type of customer who wanted to drive a 911 had changed. New customers wanted high performance but they wanted comfort, too. The general look and feel of the 911 had not kept up with the times. It was still firmly rooted in the 1960s. Yes, over the course of the years, constant improvements had been made but, from a commercial standpoint, its possibilities had pretty much been exhausted. What was needed was a modern vehicle which could stand up to the competition. This was the design brief for the Type 964. At Porsche there was no shortage in the expertise and experience needed. The company's experience in production of prototype and small series vehicles, like the 959, was notable.

The 964 sported numerous new features, not previously available on the classic 911. For example, it was the first standard production Porsche to have all-wheel-drive, employing a simplified version of the technology previously used on the 959. In addition, it was the first vehicle in which Porsche abandoned the use of rear torsion bars on the suspension that it had used on the 356 and 911 models for 40 years. The 964 had completely new light alloy suspension with telescopic McPherson struts in the front and coil springs at the rear. Power steering and ABS were standard. The new 3.6-liter engine had twin-spark ignition, knock control and a three-way catalytic converter.

The car's exterior was redesigned, too. It differed from the G model in numerous aspects. Foremost among these was the new look of the front and rear bumpers. They were markedly more substantial than those on the earlier 911s. Thanks to the improved aerodynamics and the undertray fairing, the car achieved a drag factor of 0.32, lower than that of any 911. Thus equipped, the 250-hp 964 reached the same top speed of 162 mph (260 km/h) as the 911 Turbo (the 50-hp Type 930) of the old G Series. A new rear spoiler, that raised automatically at speeds above 50 mph (80 km/h), took the place of the older fixed spoiler and was available as an optional on all the Carrera models. This improved not only the car's aerodynamics, but also its engine cooling. Initially, the only 964 to be offered alongside the 911 Carrera 3.2 with the original 911 body was the all-wheel drive Carrera 4 version.

Porsche continued using the well-established six-cylinder, air-cooled, dry sump lubrication boxer engine for the 964 as well, but further updated it with the addition of twin-spark ignition and a Bosch DME electronic engine management system.

The extra 400 cc brought the total displacement to 3.6 liters, making it possible for the engine to deliver 250 hp at 6,100 rpm. A DME with integrated knock control that automatically adjusted the ignition as a function of different fuel grades was an another new feature. This, together with the car's improved aerodynamics, significantly reduced the fuel consumption in comparison with the older 3.2-liter engine.

One year later, in 1989, the year of Professor Ferdinand "Ferry" Porsche's eightieth birthday, Porsche presented the Carrera 964, a car with rear-wheel drive only and available either as a coupe, cabriolet or targa. Its Tiptronic transmission, with two shift gates for manual or automatic gear selection was another new feature. In 1990 Porsche held its first Carrera Cup.

156-157 For model-year 1991, the 964 was offered in a Turbo version as well, with a 3.3-liter, 320 hp engine. In 1993 this was upgraded to 3.6 liters and 360 hp.

Even more importantly, in October of the same year it unveiled its 911 Carrera RS at the British International Motor Show in Birmingham, UK. This car is considered by many, even today, to be the quintessential Porsche. The 911 Carrera RS was a road-going sports car with 260 hp but could be turned into a racecar with only a few modifications. Stripped down to the bare minimum the car weighed barely 2,734 lbs (1,240 kg) and could accelerate from 0 to 62 mph (0 to 100 km/h) in 5.4 seconds. A total of 2,391 examples were sold.

The top end model of the 911 Turbo, the series M, was based on the 964 and was released in the model year 1991. This version adopted many of the elements of the earlier Turbo model (930 series), such as the widened front and rear fenders and the fixed rear spoiler. The engine was still the well-established Type 930 of the previous model, but now with 320 hp thanks to an improved engine management system and a 30% larger intercooler First unveiled in September 1992, the new Type M64 power unit entered production in January 1993 and was used on the Turbo as well. The engine displacement was increased to 3.6 liters and delivered 360 hp with the same turbocharger and intercooler as the previous model. The 3.6-liter Turbo model came with a 92-liter fuel tank as a standard feature.

At the end of 1992 Porsche introduced a commemorative edition of the 964 that was especially luxurious and somewhat

158-159 The 1991 964 Turbo could accelerate from 0 to 62 mph (0 to 100 km/h) in 5 seconds and could reach a top speed of 168 mph (270 km/h).

unique in comparison with series production models. Later, in 1993 on the occasion of the 30th anniversary of the 911, Porsche released 911 units of a special series of commemorative 964 models. These vehicles were produced in model-year 1993 (P series) and 1994 (R series). The special model "911 30 Years Edition" was the all-wheel drive Carrera version of the 964 with the Turbo model's wide coupe body. The overly large rear spoiler, however, was sacrificed in the interest of a more harmonious and elegant profile. Another version of the 964 series was the Speedster, which was produced as a special edition limited to 930 units and was based on the 964 Carrera 2 Cabriolet platform with a low raked windshield, a modified roof structure and the twin headrest hump tail, its most distinctive feature. By special customer request, Porsche's Exclusive Workshop also produced approximately 15 units of the Speedster with the optional Turbo-look wide-bodies.

In 1993 the Porsche lineup was extended with approximately 90 sports racing units of the 300-hp 911 Carrera RS 3.8 and 911 Carrera RSR 3.8. These vehicles were developed by the Weissach Racing Department. This was a car with a 3.7 liter, six-cylinder boxer engine, a Turbo-style wide-body and three-part Speedline wheels which some 911 fans came to regard as by far the best looking sports car of the Carrera RS and 964 series. Unlike the standard RS models, these cars featured aluminum doors.

160-161 *The windshield on this Speedster was firmly glued to the body, while the soft top barely deserved to be called a top. Anyway, no one drove the Speedster with the soft top up.*

162-163 *The 911 Carrera 2 Speedster was introduced in 1992 and was available only with rear-wheel drive.*

Porsche 911 – 993

In 1993 a new generation of the 911 was introduced: the 993. The design of the 964, as it was, had never been fully embraced by some Porsche enthusiasts who considered its fenders too bulky, despite the fact that it still embodied the fundamental traits of the classic 911. The smooth bumper shields, further integrated into the vehicle's body, were supposed to take care of this perceived flaw, imparting the expected elegance to the vehicle. Harm Lagaay, its chief designer, had been inspired in his design by the original model, in which the bumpers flowed smoothly into the car's overall profile to form an aesthetically harmonious unity. The light strip across the vehicle's rear end was tilted even further and, in combination with the strongly flared rear wheel arches, made for a successful design.

The standard Carrera models came with a 3.6-liter, air-cooled, six-cylinder boxer engine delivering 272 hp at 6,100 rpm. Top speed was 168 mph (270 km/h). A 286-hp model was also available. The running gear was also notably improved with larger brakes with drilled discs, an optimized ABS 5 system, and rear tires that were widened by 0.8 in. (20 mm).

Initially the 993 was offered only in two versions - a rear-wheel drive Carrera and an all-wheel drive Carrera 4. Starting in March 1994 the 911 (993) was also available as a cabriolet. Its soft top was completely automatic and could open and close in 13 seconds. It featured the new Tiptronic S with rocker switches incorporated in the steering wheel. At the end of the year Porsche introduced the Carrera 4S, a sort of cross between the Carrera 4 and the Turbo. The 4S sported the Turbo's front bumper shield. Its rear axle was 2.4 in. (6 cm) wider than that of the Carrera and the rear fenders were widened accordingly. Standard equipment included the 18-inch wheels and the Turbo's red calipers.

The 993 3.8 Cup, based on the Porsche 993, made its debut in the 1994 Porsche Supercup Championship and, one year later, was also entered in the Carrera Cup Championship. This vehicle was much improved, and was much faster and easier

to handle compared to the previous Carrera 2 (964). Credit for this was largely due to the new multi-link rear suspension. Power was unleashed through a six-speed manual transmission. The boxer engine's capacity was increased to 3.8 liters, and the 310 hp made it possible for the vehicle to reach a top speed of about 174 mph (280 km/h).

The new 993 Turbo was introduced in 1995. Its 3.6-liter, six-cylinder engine, equipped for the first time with two turbo-chargers, developed 408 hp. Unlike the previous 964 series model, the Turbo 993 came with twin turbochargers and two intercoolers, thereby guaranteeing a faster response and a more uniform power output. By now the characteristic turbo-lag of turbo engines had been more or less completely eliminated, and power output was no longer subject to the sudden surge associated with the earlier turbo's short delay in responding to pressure applied to the accelerator pedal. Unlike the previous version, the Turbo 993 came with all-wheel drive but, like the 964, it made do without twin-spark ignition. Because of the longer intake tubes across the turbochargers and the related intercoolers, the sound of the turbocharged engine sound was different to that of the standard aspirated Carrera engine. It was less aggressive.

The first GT2 was also introduced in 1995. This was a lightweight version of the Carrera. It was designed both for road use and racing and developed between 430 and 600 hp (Turbo). After a gap of a couple of years it also became available in the Targa version even if, for all intents and purposes, this was just a 911 Carrera with a wide, glass roof.

Also in this year, an extremely sporty Carrera RS was added to the lineup. Aesthetically, it was vastly different from the standard version, and with just a few modifications it could easily be converted into a racecar. The vehicle weighed only 2,800 lbs (1,270 kg). Displacement had been increased to 3.8 liters and the engine developed 300 hp.

In 1996 the 911 GT1 racecar was introduced. It competed in three races and was victorious in all three.

The 993 series is one of the most loved and sought after series among Porsche fans. It comes as no surprise that a used 993 commands a high price.

For homologation purposes, the car had to be produced in a road-going version as well, so a small-series was produced with a 3.2-liter turbo engine that developed 544 hp and reached a top speed of 193 mph (310 km/h).

For the 1997 model-year the 993 model lineup was further extended with the Carrera S, produced in model years 1997 and 1998. The Carrera S had the same bodywork and equipment as Carrera 4S. Technically, the only differences between the two were that the Carrera S did not have all-wheel drive, the suspension or the large brakes of the 4S. Outwardly, the Carrera S was made clearly recognizable, distinguishing it from the Carrera 4S, by having its name, "Carrera S," written in steel gray letters across the engine cover. The biggest difference between it and the Carrera 4S, however, was in the split spoiler grill which was painted to match the body color. In all, 3,714 units were produced. Given that it was the last 911 to have an air-cooled engine, the 993 occupies a special place in Porsche history.

166-167 The 993 design was the work of Harm Lagaay. Initially, the new look was met with considerable alarm inasmuch as the 993 was quite a bit larger than the 964, while its bumpers didn't seem to have grown in a commensurate manner.

168-169 and 170-171 Porsche produced a small number of road-going versions of the 993 GT1 racing version. Weighing only 2,535 lbs (1,150 kg), its performance was extraordinary. It accelerated from 0 to 62 mph (0 to 100 km/h) in 3.5 seconds and reached a top speed of 193 mph (310 km/h).

Porsche GT2

The GT2 was the peak of the evolution of the 911 as a sports car. A turbo, but with higher performance, greater torque and available only with rear wheel drive. Although a racecar, it was homologated for road use. The GT2 name, in line with the FIA regulations, was officially used only for the first series (993). Starting in 2000, in fact, GT2s should have competed only in a higher power class, but Porsche decided to keep the name as by then it had already become something of a cult.

The 911 Turbo S Le Mans GT was a single unit produced especially for the Le Mans race and based on the 911 Turbo (964). According to the design files it was a competitive version of the Turbo, guaranteeing improved performance thanks to better power-to-weight ratio, a direct result of the stripped down equipment and redesigned layout.

The first generation of the 911 GT2 was introduced in 1995 and was based on the 911 Turbo (993). Thanks to the updated M64/60 engine, it was renamed M64/60 R, and produced 430 hp at 5,750 rpm and a maximum torque of 398 lb.-ft. (540 Nm) at 4,500 rpm. In all, 172 units of this version were produced, enough to obtain homologation. The racing version in 1995 with 330 kW (450 hp), and in 1998 with 345 kW (485 hp) at 5,750 rpm, not to mention 490 lb.-ft. (665 Nm), was called the 911 GT2 R. The new model, still based on the 993 Turbo, and introduced in 1998, was the last car in the 911 GT2 series to be air-cooled. It produced 450 hp at 5,750 rpm with a maximum torque of 432 lb.-ft. (585 Nm) at 4,500 rpm. With a curb weight of 2,855 lbs (1,295 kg), this GT2 streaked from 0 to 62 mph (0 to 100 km) in 4.1 seconds and attained a top speed of 186 mph (300 km/h). In the end only 21 units were sold. The 600 hp racing version, equipped with twin KKK model K27 turbochargers was sold to private teams as a 911 GT2 Evolution from 1995 to 1997.

172-173 The 996 series Porsche GT2 was a version of the 911 produced exclusively for road use. It was the first Porsche fitted with carbon-fiber composite ceramic brakes as a standard feature.

Unlike the previous air-cooled model, the GT2 series was built exclusively for road use. However, it still had a lot of racecar-derived components, like the adjustable shock absorbers, the wheelbase and the toe and camber. The 996 GT2 and 911 GT3 series also came in Clubsport versions. They were the first Porsches to come with carbon-fiber composite ceramic brakes as a standard feature. Compared to the 420 hp Turbo model, the GT2 produced 462 hp, with a maximum torque of 457 lb.-ft. (620 Nm), in the 3,500–4,500 rpm range. Thus equipped, the vehicle, which weighed 3,175 lbs (1,440 kg), accelerated from 0 to 62 mph (0 to 100 km/h) in 4.1 seconds and reached a top speed of 196 mph (315 km/h). Between the fall of 2000 and spring of 2003, 963 units were sold. Starting in April 2003, Porsche offered its clients an updated version that did not look any different on the outside from the previous model, but delivered 483 hp at 5,700 rpm with a maximum torque of 472 lb.-ft. (640 Nm) in the 3,500–4,500 rpm range. The curb weight was reduced to 3,131 lbs (1,420 kg).

At the 2007 Frankfurt IAA the 997 series GT2 was introduced with an output of 530 hp at 6,500 rpm and a maximum torque of 502 lb.-ft. (680 Nm) available in the 2,200–4,500 rpm range. With acceleration from 0 to 62 mph (0 to 100 km/h) in 3.7 seconds and a top speed of 204 mph (329 km/h), the GT2 997, weighing 3,340 lbs (1,515 kg), was the fastest and most powerful 911 in the series. But there was clearly room for improvement. In 2010 Porsche introduced the GT2 RS, a timely revised version of the GT2, limited to 500 units, and equipped with a boxer, six-cylinder, twin-turbo engine. It delivered 620 hp and its curb weight was further reduced to 3,020 lbs (1,370 kg), thanks to the use of carbon-fiber composite materials. Official figures for the GT2 RS are 3.5 seconds to accelerate from 0 to 62 mph (0 to 100 km/h), 9.4 seconds to reach 124 mph (200 km/h), and 26.7 seconds for the dream threshold of 186 mph (300 km/h). The top speed was electronically limited to 205 mph (330 km/h).

174-175 Starting in April 2003, Porsche offered an upgraded version (MK2) with power output and torque further upgraded to 483 hp and 472 lb.-ft. (640 Nm), respectively.

175 The first water-cooled GT2 was unveiled in August 2000 at the North American International Auto Show. Compared to the 420-hp 996 Turbo, it produced 462 hp (a 10% increase) and a maximum torque of 457 lb.-ft. (620 Nm).

176-177 *The 911 GT2 of the 997 series was presented in 2007 at the Frankfurt IAA. A power output of 530 hp and a maximum torque of 502 lb.-ft. (680 Nm) made it the fastest 911 ever produced at that time.*

Porsche Boxster

178-179 *The first Boxsters were a disappointment. With just 204 hp they just weren't powerful enough compared to the preceding model, the 968 Cabrio.*

180-181 *When it came to the Boxster, Porsche clearly looked to its glorious past for inspiration. Take the side air intakes for example.*

To call the reception which greeted the model introduced in 1996 as enthusiastic would undoubtedly be a gross exaggeration. Porsche had already had some experience with the cool reception of a new model. The 924 and 928, for example, had certainly not been welcomed with open arms by Porsche enthusiasts, even though sales of these models were certainly up to the mark. The problem was by no means one of design. The Boxster Concept, first introduced at the Detroit Auto Show in 1993, had very pleasing lines, a good mix of retro references to the 550 Spyder and 718 RS 60, as well as modern elements. The Boxster's problem was not unlike the one that afflicts all car companies that introduce a model that is just one notch below the level of their traditional core business. Enthusiasts immediately criticized its lack of power. In its first years, in fact, the Boxster didn't have much to offer in that regard. The 2.5-liter, six-cylinder, mid-mounted engine barely produced 204 hp. On the flip side, the Boxster weighed only 2,756 lbs (1,250 kg) and could reach a maximum speed of 149 mph (240 km/h), even if one certainly couldn't have called it a powerhouse. With a base price of 76,500 marks (about 43,000 GBP), the Boxster may not have been exactly a good deal, but it nevertheless attracted a new class of customer. It wasn't long, in fact, before it was nicknamed the "hairdresser's Porsche."

Initially the Boxster was made in Stuttgart, but in 1997 Valmet Automotive, in the Finnish town of Uuisikaupunki, also began production. Notwithstanding numerous requests from customers, Porsche failed to upgrade the power output of the car's engine until the year 2000, and even then it wasn't a significant increase. The engine displacement was upgraded to 2.7 liters with 220 hp. At the same time, a new model, the Boxster S, was introduced with a 3.2-liter engine delivering 252 hp. Thus equipped, the Boxster could at last be defined as a true sports car. Shortly before its introduction, additional features were added, such as a new Motronic engine control system and the VarioCam, which increased the power of the S model to 260 hp and the power of the base model to 228 hp. For 2004 Porsche introduced a really unusual model, the "550 Spyder 50 Year Anniversary Edition", with 266 hp, available only in silver. A total of 1,953 units were sold.

The 2004 model-year was based on the new generation 987 series, which replaced the 986. The main difference was the disappearance of the "fried egg" style light cluster in favor of new headlights that were similar to those of the 911. Another plus was the powered soft top, which could be operated not only when the car was stationary, but also at speeds of up to 31 mph (50 km/h). The debut of the new model was of course accompanied by a slight increase in power output, 240 hp for the base model and 280 hp for the S model. In mid-2006 this was upgraded again to 245 hp and 295 hp, respectively.

182-183 When it comes to finding the right name for a car the discussions go on and on, forever. Is it a cabrio, a roadster or a spider/spyder? With a Porsche you can't go wrong. The answer is simply: 'a Boxster'.

The special model "RS 60 Spyder," inspired by the racing model 718 RS 60, produced as much as 303 hp. 1,960 units were made. Thanks to direct fuel injection, starting in 2009 the base version of the Boxster produced 255 hp, and the S version produced 310 hp. Starting in 2011, three Boxsters, equipped exclusively with electric engines, were also tested on the roads around Stuttgart.

The Boxster Spyder introduced in 2009 was really very exciting. Its 320-hp engine and 2,800-lb (1,270-kg) curb weight made its performance the sportiest of all the Porsche models. The two-part canvas top, on the other hand, was perhaps the most absurd top ever seen on a car. Only a professional camper would have been capable of installing or removing it. This feature, as well as the steep price, may explain why only 1,667 units of this interesting model were sold. The online review www.radical-mag.com wrote:

"Is the Spyder really any more beautiful? Was it really necessary to make it so complicated? Was there not a more elegant solution? Does a design change always translate to a better product? If everything has to be so extravagant and unusual, why didn't the Stuttgart team just do away with the roof altogether? It's fair to suppose that customers will drive this car with the roof removed, if only because it's the only practical solution. Furthermore, Porsche only guarantees this camping equipment

at speeds up to 124 mph (200 km/h); at higher speeds you have to drive without the top on. Of course, when all is said and done one can get used to anything, especially as, once the car's proud owner will have removed and replaced the soft top of the Porsche Boxster Spyder for the 169th time, he will surely have learned all the tricks he needs to know to handle its canvas, how to avoid spraining his fingers in the process, and in what sequence to undo all the tie rods, etc."

The third generation Boxster, called the 981 series, was introduced in April 2012. For both versions, the power output was increased by 10 hp and the wheelbase was extended by 2.4 in. (6 cm). Despite this, the weight was reduced by approximately 110 lbs (50 kg), resulting in improved fuel consumption, thanks also in part to its new Start-Stop system. The design was improved as well. The third generation's profile was sleeker and more elegant. Another quote from www.radical-mag.com states:

"We don't understand all this fuss about the new Boxster. They say it's better than the 911: it isn't true, once and for all. It's the 911's younger sister, destined to belong to all those who can't afford the original, and who probably couldn't handle it if they were to find themselves behind its wheel. No, the Boxster is not a car for pin-ups, and is no longer the hairdresser's version of the 911: it simply became a better car. But... There is nothing to add."

184-185 In 2009 Porsche brought out an orange "Limited Edition" Boxster designed exclusively for the North American market. It was based both on the 2.7- liter and the S version.

186-187 The front light clusters of the Boxster were highly reminiscent of those of the 911. Probably too much so, suggesting a lack of new ideas.

184-185 In 2009 Porsche brought out an orange "Limited Edition" Boxster designed exclusively for the North American market. It was based both on the 2.7- liter and the S version.

186-187 The front light clusters of the Boxster were highly reminiscent of those of the 911. Probably too much so, suggesting a lack of new ideas.

188, 188-189 and 190-191 The third generation Boxster (known in-house as the 981) was introduced in 2012 and was longer with the wheelbase being extended by 3.9 in. (10 cm). Despite this, it weighed approximately 110 lbs (50 kg) less.

192 The GTS is the most sporty of the Boxster series. This version was introduced in 2014.

193 With its 330 hp and dual-clutch transmission (optional), the Boxster GTS can accelerate from 0 to 62 mph (0 to 100 km/h) in 4.7 seconds.

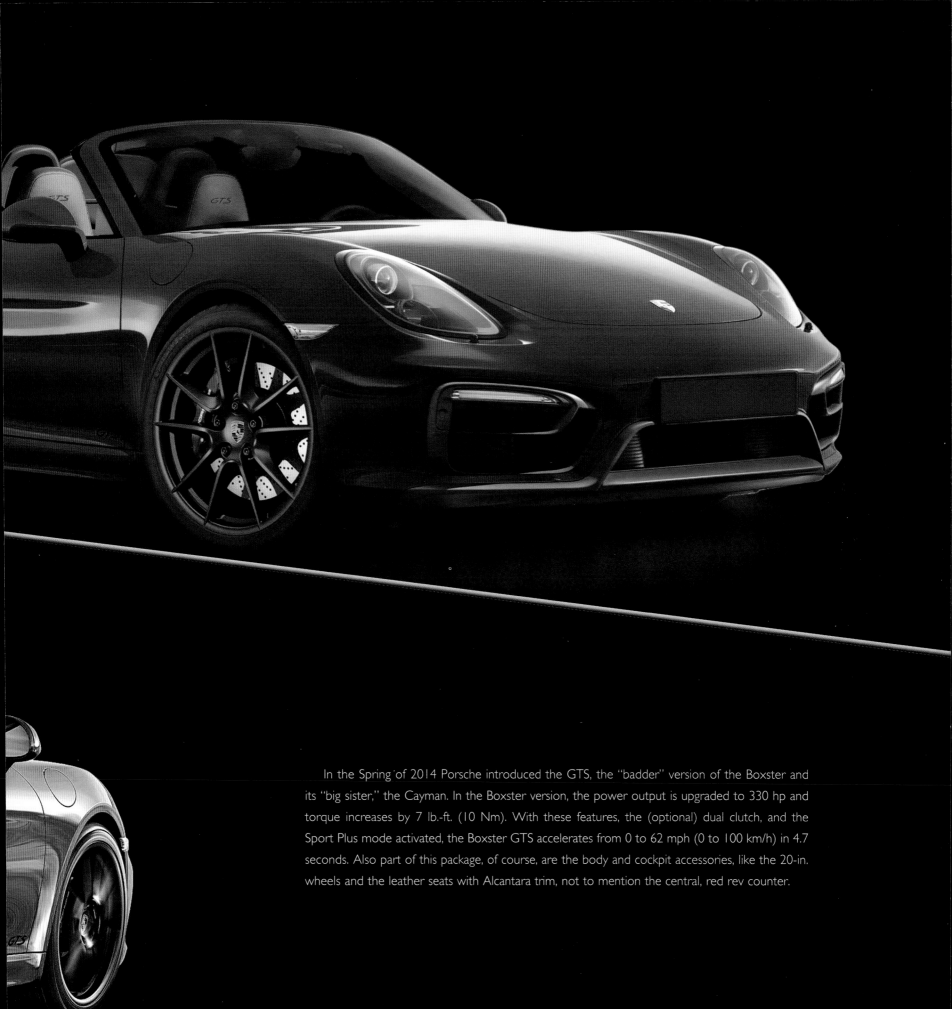

In the Spring of 2014 Porsche introduced the GTS, the "badder" version of the Boxster and its "big sister," the Cayman. In the Boxster version, the power output is upgraded to 330 hp and torque increases by 7 lb.-ft. (10 Nm). With these features, the (optional) dual clutch, and the Sport Plus mode activated, the Boxster GTS accelerates from 0 to 62 mph (0 to 100 km/h) in 4.7 seconds. Also part of this package, of course, are the body and cockpit accessories, like the 20-in. wheels and the leather seats with Alcantara trim, not to mention the central, red rev counter.

The six-cylinder 996 engines were similar to those used in the Boxster, but the only thing they had in common with the air-cooled engines of the previous 911 models was the number of cylinders. The place of the earlier dry sump lubrication with a separate oil tank was taken by a dry sump with an oil reservoir in the engine. In place of the twin-spark ignition used in the earlier 993 series, the 996 was equipped with static high-voltage distribution with six ignition modules.

The DOHC engine block was decidedly more complex than that of air-cooled engines where the block consisted of two halves and had only two timing chains. The new blocks were four-piece and had four camshafts driven by a total of five chains. These included a duplex row roller chain that drove an intermediate shaft located underneath the crankshaft. Two duplex row roller chains (one in front of and one behind the engine) connected this first chain to the exhaust camshafts. These in turn, controlled the corresponding intake camshafts by means of a single row roller chain that worked with a variable camshaft control (VarioCam).

When it first came onto the market, the Porsche 996 had a 3,387 cc (3.4 liter) engine that developed 300 hp at 6,800 rpm. In contrast to the models that preceded it, the body of the 996 was no longer based on Ferdinand Alexander Porsche's 1963 design. It was lengthened by 7.5 in. (19 cm) and widened by 3.7 in. (9.5 cm). The light clusters built into the fenders, often referred to as 'fried egg' lights, were its most distinctive feature and were borrowed from the Boxster to cut costs. The car's interior was also completely revamped. The most obvious change was to the instrument panel. The rev counter continued to occupy the central position and to be dominant because it was the largest instrument. The other four dials were arranged differently, in a semicircle like the Boxster dash. The speedometer and the voltmeter were to the left of the rev counter. The water temperature gauge and the fuel and oil pressure gauges were to the right of the rev counter. Because customers had often complained about how difficult it was to read the instruments, especially the speedometer, the road speed was now displayed in analog and digital format in both the speedometer and the rev counter. The central console and interior door trim were also redesigned. All the interior elements had a coordinated design. Many Porsche enthusiasts do not consider the vehicles that came after the 996 series to be the real thing, they are not, so to speak, 'genuine' 911s.

194-195 The Porsche 911 996 series was produced between 1997 and 2006. It was the first 911 model to come with a water-cooled engine.

The twin turbo engine with its two intercoolers had a displacement of 3,600 cc (3.6 liter) and, in contrast to the Carrera model engines, had an external oil tank for the dry sump lubrication. It was also equipped with the VarioCam Plus system that used a combination of variable valve timing and valve-lift. A five-speed Tiptronic S transmission was available as an optional. With the manual gearbox the vehicle could accelerate from 0 to 62 mph (0 to 100 km/h) in 4.2 seconds.

196-197 Harm Lagaay led the design team on the new 996. In comparison with all the preceding models of the 911, this was the one whose design departed the furthest from Ferdinand Alexander Porsche's original design.

Starting with model-year 2002, the engine capacity of the 911 was increased to 3,596 cc (3.6 liter) with an accompanying upgrade of horsepower to 320 at the same rpm. From the end of 2001, the X50 power upgrade package was also available. This pushed the power output to 450 hp at 5,700 rpm and the maximum torque to 457 lb.-ft. (620 Nm) in the 3,500 to 4,500 rpm range. The increased power was the result of larger turbochargers (K24 instead of K16), more efficient intercoolers and a higher maximum boost pressure (0.9 bars instead of 0.8). Different catalytic converters and exhaust pipes also helped. In addition, the electronic control unit was upgraded and the gearbox was reinforced with roller bearings.

Top of the range was the GT2. Its 3,600 cc, six-cylinder, twin-turbo boxer engine was based on the race proven '98 GT1. It developed 462 hp. Maximum torque of 457 lb.-ft. (620 Nm) was available between 3,500 and 4,500 rpm. Its top speed was 196 mph (315 km/h).

In 2002 the power output of the 911 Carrera 2 was upgraded to 320 hp. The engine capacity was increased from 3.2 to 3.4 liters and the body styling was slightly revised.

198-199 The 996 was also available as a Cabriolet, a fact that was not particularly appreciated by fans of the traditional 911.

After a four-year gap, Porsche offered the 911 Targa again, this one featuring a glass roof. Another new model was the Carrera 4S, which combined the naturally aspirated Carrera engine with the wide-body style of the 911 Turbo.

In 2003 a commemorative edition was produced for the 40th anniversary of the 911. This version was based on the 996 platform, but had an additional 25 hp, bringing the total power output to 345 hp. The paintwork was a special silver gray previously only available on the Carrera GT. The front-end was styled like the 4S and Turbo models. The high-gloss polished 18-inch wheels, optional on all other 996 series models, were standard. The vehicle, of which a total of 1,963 units were produced, had an exclusive stylish interior.

In 2003 Porsche introduced another two versions of the 911 - the 911 Carrera 4S Cabriolet and the 911 Turbo Cabriolet. The GT3 also became available again, this time with 381 hp. This car could accelerate from 0 to 62 mph (0 to 100 km/h) in 4.5 seconds and reach a top speed of 190 mph (306 km/h). Two hundred, road-going examples of the 911 GT3 RS were produced; this car later served as the base model for competition vehicles.

Porsche GT3

To purists and real aficionados alike, the only *true* 911 is the GT3. Like the GT2 it was a car whose origins could be traced directly to motorsport, but it had a classic naturally-aspirated engine. In other words, no turbocharger and no all-wheel drive. The words which best describe this car are - lightweight, powerful and lots and lots of driving pleasure.

The first GT3 came on the market in 1999 as a series 996. It was the first sportscar model of the Porsche 911 series to be equipped with a water-cooled, naturally-aspirated engine. Porsche adopted the GT3 name from the racing category in which the racing version would later compete in endurance races. Its bodywork was based on the shell of the Porsche 911 Carrera 4, the all-wheel drive version of the 996 series. Because the GT3 was rear-wheel drive, and thanks also to the elimination of the front differential and spare tire, the fuel tank could be increased from a 16.9-gallon (64-liter) to a 23.5-gallon (89-liter) capacity. From the outside, the GT3 (996) differed from the Carrera in its revised front apron, which had an added rubber lip, and in the new look of the door sills. But the most striking difference was the "bi-plane" rear spoiler, whose angle could be adjusted to six different positions, thereby guaranteeing optimal configuration whether for regular on-road driving or for the race track.

Under its hood the GT3 sported the well-known 3.6-liter flat six, now improved with dry sump lubrication. The compression ratio was slightly increased from 11.3:1 to 11.7:1, while the redline was at 7,800 rpm, enabling the engine to develop

360 hp and a maximum torque of 273 lb.-ft. (370 Nm) at 5,000 rpm. Thanks to a weight of barely 2,976 lbs (1,350 kg), the first GT3 accelerated from 0 to 62 mph (0 to 100 km/h) in 4.8 seconds and was also the first 911 series 996 to reach a top speed of 186 mph (300 km/h). The car had the 6-speed manual transmission of the GT2. In all, 1,350 units were made.

This first GT3 was also available at no extra cost in a Clubsport version. Among other things, this version came with a painted bolt-on roll bar built into the cockpit, fire-resistant seat covers and red Schroth seatbelts. The driver got a six-point racing harness. In this version, the side airbags had to be sacrificed, but the doors were further reinforced in compensation.

Following the success of the 911 GT3, Porsche designed a second one, this one based on the now-updated 996 series. This version became available in April 2003. Its engine developed 381 hp at 7,400 rpm (the redline was at 8,200 rpm). The new GT3 differed from the first series in its teardrop-shaped light cluster, borrowed from the 996 Turbo, a signature look of all 996 Porsches that were made after the fall of 2001. The shape of the back spoiler, often described as an 'ironing board' was also different. This second generation was slightly faster than the first, at least on paper, but also 66 lbs (30 kg) heavier – something which did not sit well with the purists. The lighter version would be the Clubsport, the now-famed 911 GT3 RS. While the weight was shaved by just 44 lbs (20 kg), Porsche enthusiasts immediately fell in love with it. A rally version of the GT3 was also available on request.

202-203 The 997 series GT3 RS was introduced in 2006 and produced until 2009. Its engine developed 415 hp and the vehicle weighed 44 lbs. (20 kg) less than the GT3.

torque of 299 lb.-ft. (405 Nm) was reached at 5,500 rpm. The maximum torque could be boosted by 18 lb.-ft. (25 Nm) by pressing the "Sport" button in the central console. The car would then rocket from 0 to 62 mph (0 a 100 km/h) in 4.3 seconds. Top speed was 186 mph (310 km/h).

As expected, the GT3 997 was later also available in an RS version. The engine was unchanged, but the vehicle weighed 44 lbs (20 kg) less than the standard GT3, thanks to the use of carbon fiber in the adjustable rear spoiler and the use of plastics in the rear window and engine hood. The vehicle was also 1.7 in (44 mm) wider at the rear axle.

204-205 The standard 997 series GT3 was advertised by Porsche as 'pure science.' For the first time, Porsche was able to optimize aerodynamics on a standard production vehicle to the point where the car didn't create any lift at all.

In 2009, a year after the Carrera versions, the GT3 997 series also underwent a restyling. The engine size was increased from 3.6 to 3.8 liters and the power output reached 435 hp but, in contrast to the Carrera and Turbo versions, it didn't have direct fuel injection. As in the restyling of the 996 series GT3, the rear bi-plane spoiler was substituted with a single spoiler.

In April 2011 the 911 GT3 RS 4.0 was introduced. Its production was limited to 600 units. This vehicle was powered by a 4.0-liter, 6-cylinder boxer engine that developed 500 hp and a maximum torque of 339 lb.-ft. (460 Nm). This was the 911 GT3's highest performance engine ever in terms of both engine size and power. At 2,998 lbs (1,360 kg) curb weight it was 22 lbs (10 kg) lighter than the GT3 RS 3.8 which, along with the GT3 3.8, went out of production upon introduction of the 911 GT3 RS 4.0.

A GT3 version was also designed for the more recent 991 platform of the 911. This vehicle had rear-wheel drive, menacing fixed spoilers, imposing wheels with central locking wheel nuts and an engine that had previously seemed to be destined to disappear altogether. This power unit was a naturally-aspirated DOC (diesel oxidation catalyst, no longer based on the refined Mezger engine which retired with dignity along with the RS 4.0, but on the newer direct fuel injection (DFI) engine. But there was no need to worry, because even the new GT3 came with a thoroughbred racing engine which, aside from the oil sump, did not use a single component of the engine fitted to the Carrera, from its crankshaft, to the completely-revised cylinder head, to the titanium connecting rods attached to forged pistons.

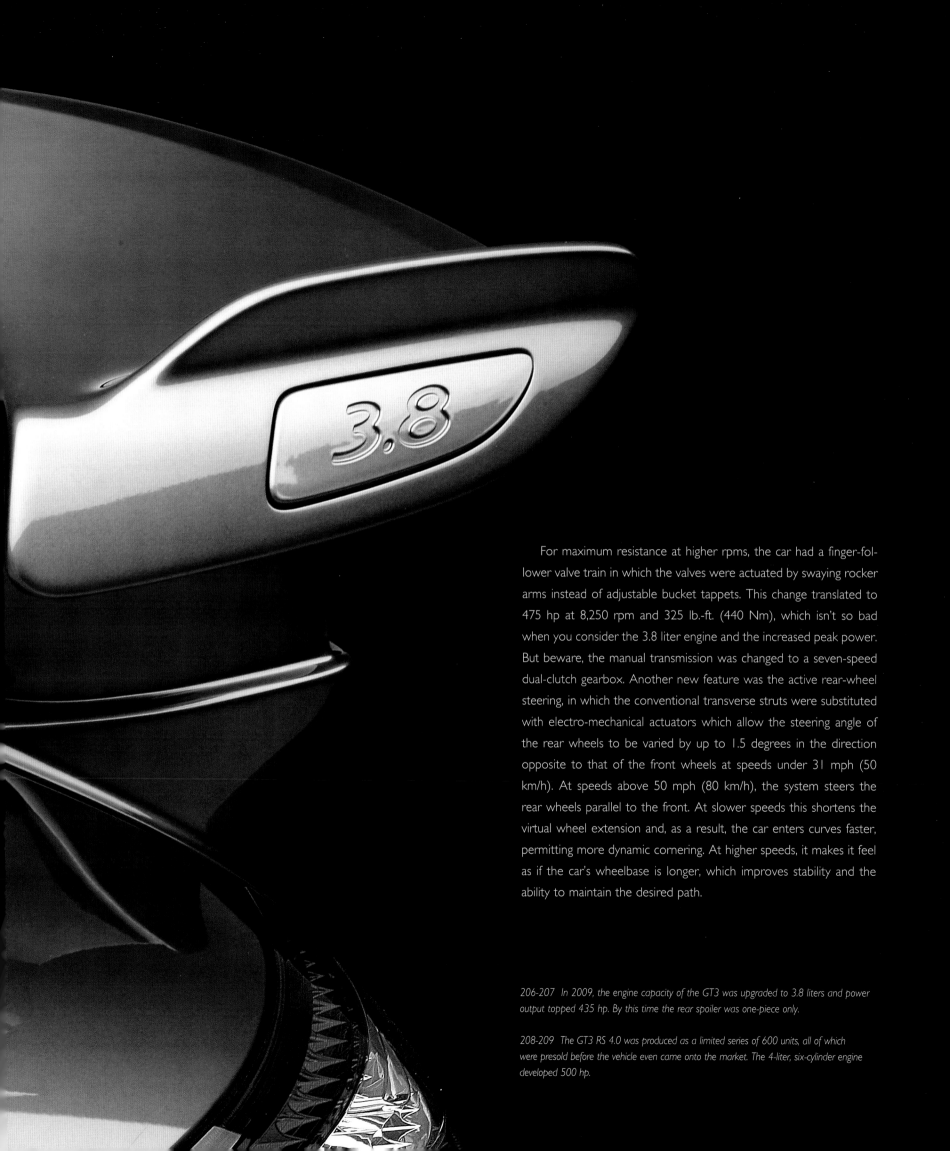

For maximum resistance at higher rpms, the car had a finger-follower valve train in which the valves were actuated by swaying rocker arms instead of adjustable bucket tappets. This change translated to 475 hp at 8,250 rpm and 325 lb.-ft. (440 Nm), which isn't so bad when you consider the 3.8 liter engine and the increased peak power. But beware, the manual transmission was changed to a seven-speed dual-clutch gearbox. Another new feature was the active rear-wheel steering, in which the conventional transverse struts were substituted with electro-mechanical actuators which allow the steering angle of the rear wheels to be varied by up to 1.5 degrees in the direction opposite to that of the front wheels at speeds under 31 mph (50 km/h). At speeds above 50 mph (80 km/h), the system steers the rear wheels parallel to the front. At slower speeds this shortens the virtual wheel extension and, as a result, the car enters curves faster, permitting more dynamic cornering. At higher speeds, it makes it feel as if the car's wheelbase is longer, which improves stability and the ability to maintain the desired path.

206-207 In 2009, the engine capacity of the GT3 was upgraded to 3.8 liters and power output topped 435 hp. By this time the rear spoiler was one-piece only.

208-209 The GT3 RS 4.0 was produced as a limited series of 600 units, all of which were presold before the vehicle even came onto the market. The 4-liter, six-cylinder engine developed 500 hp.

Lastly, the GT3 R Hybrid, based on the 997 and first introduced in 2010, was an unusual vehicle with overall power of 472 kW or 642 hp. Its flat six cylinder developed 480 hp and the remaining 120 kW were provided by two electric motors mounted on the front axle. Instead of a high-tension battery to store this energy, the Porsche 997 GT3 R Hybrid used a kinetic energy recovery system (KERS) developed by Williams Hybrid Power (WHP) for the Williams Formula 1 Team. This flywheel-based storage system utilized a rotor that could be electrically accelerated to speeds up to 40,000 rpm. Recharge took place during braking, thanks to the current supplied by the two electric motors mounted on the front axle (the power was equal to 2 x 60 kW). When additional energy was required during acceleration, the flywheel-based generator released it, supplying power to the two electric motors.

210-211 *The Porsche 997 GT3 R Hybrid didn't have a high-tension battery to store this energy. Instead it used a kinetic energy recovery system (KERS) developed by Williams Hybrid Power (WHP) for the Williams Formula 1 Team. Recharging took place during braking, thanks to the current supplied by the two electric motors mounted on the front axle.*

211 *In 2010 Porsche unveiled yet another unusual race car - the GT3 R Hybrid. Its flat six engine developed 480 hp. The two additional electric motors generated a further 120 kW.*

Porsche Cayenne

212 The Cayenne, introduced in 2002, is Porsche's best-selling car.

True Porsche enthusiasts cry their hearts out when faced with the Cayenne. The SUV is *de facto* a peripheral category of car and the very fact that Porsche should be making one is a lamentable fact in itself and nothing to be proud of. However, it's been so financially profitable for the Stuttgart company that one must put up with it. This is good news because it's allowed Porsche to design other cars far more winning than this pseudo off-roader. Besides, the Cayenne isn't really a Porsche. It's a joint project between Porsche, Volkswagen (Touareg) and Audi (Q7). Just one year after it was first introduced, the Cayenne was already the most widely sold Porsche model.

The 9P series was unveiled in 2002 and remained in production until 2010. In 2007 it underwent modest restyling. The car came in a variety of power versions. A 3.2-liter V6 with 250 hp (thus equipped, one couldn't exactly describe this almost 2.2 short ton/2 metric ton colossal vehicle as excessively powerful) and a 4.5-liter V8 that developed 350 hp in the S version and 450 hp in the Turbo, with an optional "WLS" package that developed 500 hp. There was also the Turbo S version that developed 521 hp. The main changes in the restyling were in the engine sizes. The V6 was upgraded to 290 hp, the S to 385 hp, the Turbo to 500 hp and the "WLS" to 540 hp. To this lineup was added the 405-hp GTS, with a lowered ride height, and though it might seem like an oxymoron to have an SUV with a lowered ride height, the Cayenne customers didn't seem to notice. In 2008 the Turbo S appeared again with 550 hp and carbon ceramic brakes available upon request, and in 2009 yet another traditional rule was broken. The Cayenne became the first Porsche automobile available with a diesel engine, more specifically a 240-hp turbodiesel. With a (theoretical) top speed of 174 mph (280 km/h), the Turbo S was the fastest SUV in the world. A record as debatable as it was pointless also given the car's excessive fuel consumption.

213 top Special editions are a tradition at Porsche. This is the Cayenne Transsyberia, available in several versions.

213 bottom The Cayenne shares numerous features with the Volkswagen Touareg and the Audi Q7. As a result, production costs are significantly reduced.

primarily from the 9PA in its smaller front air vents and Panamera-like light clusters. The new Cayenne was also 2 in. (5 cm) longer than the previous version,
and its wheelbase was 1.6 in. (4 cm) longer. Despite these modifications, the
vehicle weighed 396 lbs (180 kg) less than its predecessor.

The gamut of available engines remained more or less unchanged and included the basic version, a 3.6-liter, V6 with 300 hp, the Cayenne S, a 4.8-liter,
V8 with 400 hp, the Cayenne GTS with 420 hp, the Cayenne Turbo with 500
hp, and the Cayenne Turbo S with 550 hp. In 2013 this vehicle could accelerate
from 0 to 62 mph — 0 to 100 km/h — in 4.5 seconds and reach a top speed of
176 mph —283 km/h. Later additions were the turbodiesel three-liter (245 hp)
and a new 4.2-liter, V8 diesel with 382 hp and a peak torque of 627 lb.-ft. (850
Nm), available in the fall of 2012.

214-215 In 2010 the Cayenne underwent a redesign.
The wheelbase was increased by 1.6 in. (4 cm), while the overall
length was increased by 2 in. (5 cm). The 3-liter diesel engine had
already been introduced on the previous version.

215 Since 2013 the Cayenne Turbo S boasts 550 hp
and acceleration from 0 to 62 mph (0 to 100 km/h) in 4.7
seconds.

1 High-voltage nickel–metal hydride battery
2 Air supply duct
3 Power electronics
4 Hybrid module
5 V6 3-liter compressor engine

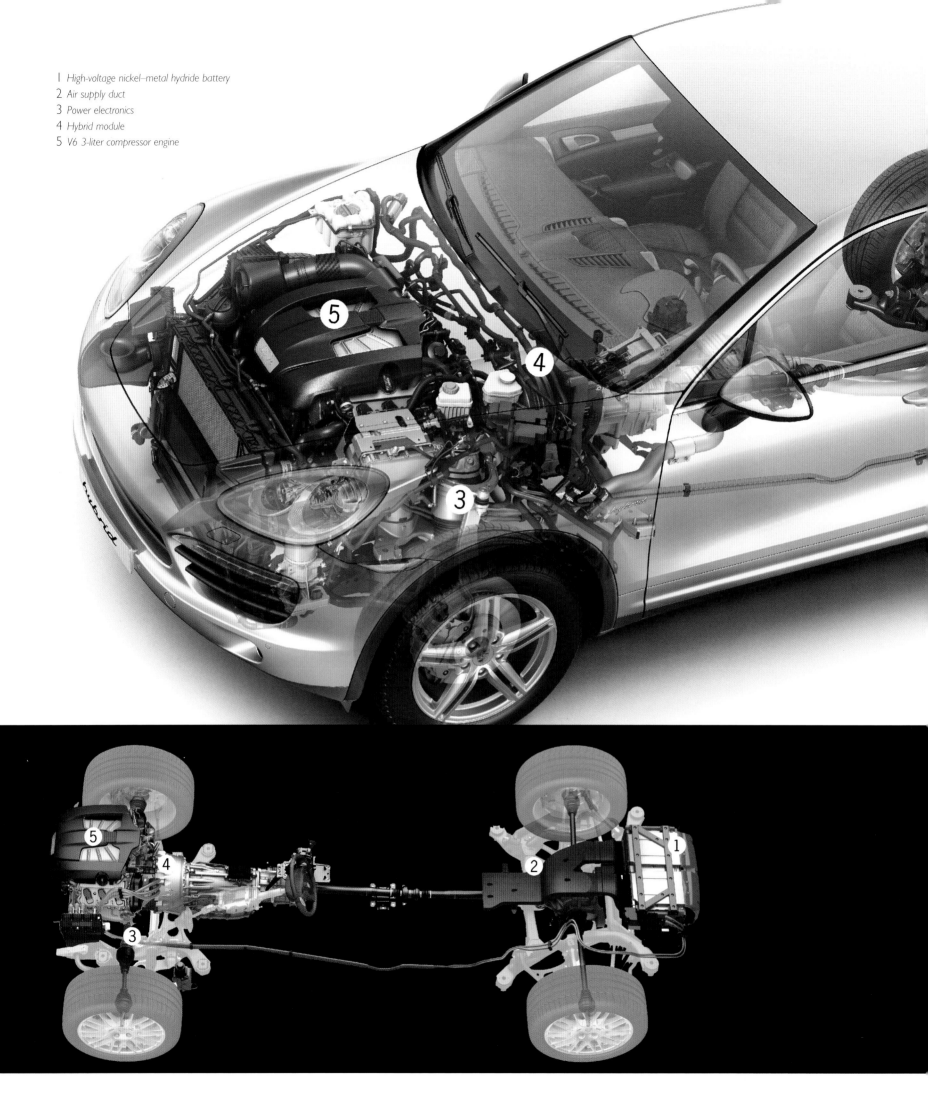

Another unprecedented edition was the Cayenne Hybrid. The hybrid drive unit consisted of a 34-kW electric motor paired with the well tried V6, 3-liter direct fuel injection engine with a volumetric turbocharger from Audi. The hybrid could produce a combined power of 333 hp with peak torque at 428 lb.-ft. (580 Nm) at just 1,000 rpm. The electric motor alone could take the vehicle up to speeds of 37 mph (60 km/h) without the assistance of the gasoline engine that could be switched off not only when the car was at a standstill, but also when the driver let up on the accelerator, in the so called sailing mode. All the Cayenne models came with automatic, eight-speed transmission.

Despite all this, the final judgment remains the same - the Cayenne, as a matter of principle, is not a *true* Porsche.

217 Available since 2010, the Cayenne S Hybrid develops 380 hp and has a fuel consumption of approx. 2.2 gal./62 mi. (8.2 liters/100 km).

Porsche Carrera GT

The Carrera GT was never intended to be a road car. Already in 1999 Porsche had wanted to return to Le Mans (the last victory had been in 1998) and had planned a vehicle for the Prototype class. Initially, this was to have been powered by a six-cylinder boxer. Later the decision was made to replace it with an unprecedented V10 whose origins went back as far as 1992 when it had been destined for the F1 Footwork Team, but was never used. In the middle of 1999, two days before it was to be track-tested, the project was shelved. Reliable sources suggest that Ferdinand Piëch, president of Volkswagen, vetoed the project because he didn't want any competition for his own "Audi-Le Mans" project, which was well underway. Moreover, many of the Porsche engineers were already tied up with development of the new Cayenne. On the other hand, they had a new engine and a new body available and management intended to use them.

This was how a new concept car, called the Carrera GT, came to be introduced at the Paris Salon of 2000. Given the considerable public interest, the supercar was introduced in 2003 and was without rivals at that time.

The Porsche Carrera GT was the first series production car built with a support frame and monocoque body made entirely of carbon-fiber composite. Even the roof, made of two removable panels that could be stowed in the trunk, was made of the same material. But the use of fancy materials did not end here. The Carrera GT tail was long because of the mid-mounted engine, and had two air vents covered with open work steel alloy. The magnesium wheels had central locking wheel nuts like those used in race cars. These were color-coded with blue for the right side and red for the left side to avoid cross-threading. A 'downforce-kit', consisting of a complex air-flow piping system in the vehicle subframe allowed the Carrera GT to take advantage of the well-known ground effect of Formula 1 to maintain stability even at high speeds. Further contributing to this was the automated rear spoiler, which automatically deployed when the car exceeded 75 mph (120 km/h), and further increased negative lift. The spoiler could also be raised manually, even when the vehicle was stationary.

218-219 The Carrera GT was produced between 2003 and 2006. Originally, a total of 1,500 units were to be produced, but production was suspended at 1,270.

The car's cockpit was designed on the "reduce to the max" principle, but not at the expense of style. The Recaro bucket seats were made of Aramid carbon fiber and weighed just under 22 lbs (10 kg). The pedals were aluminum. The gearshift lever was raised, so as to decrease the distance between it and the steering wheel, and stood out from the center console. Its ball grip was made from balsa wood, a revival of that on the famous Porsche 917.

As already mentioned, the amazing engine originated in the company's racing department. It was a 5.7-liter V10, with two overhead camshafts per cylinder bank and four valves per cylinder, producing 612 hp at 8,000 rpm and a maximum torque of 435 lb.-ft. (590 Nm) at 5,750 rpm. The vehicle — 181.6 inches long, 75.6 inches wide, and barely 45.9 inches high — rocketed from 0 to 62 mph (0 to 100 km/h) in 3.9 seconds and reached a top speed of 205 mph (334 km/h).

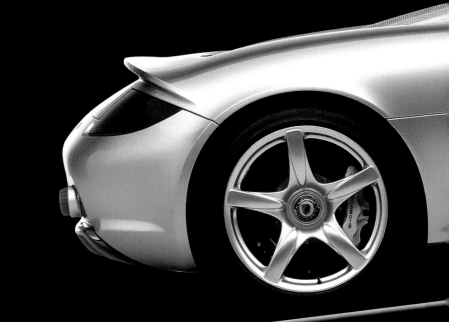

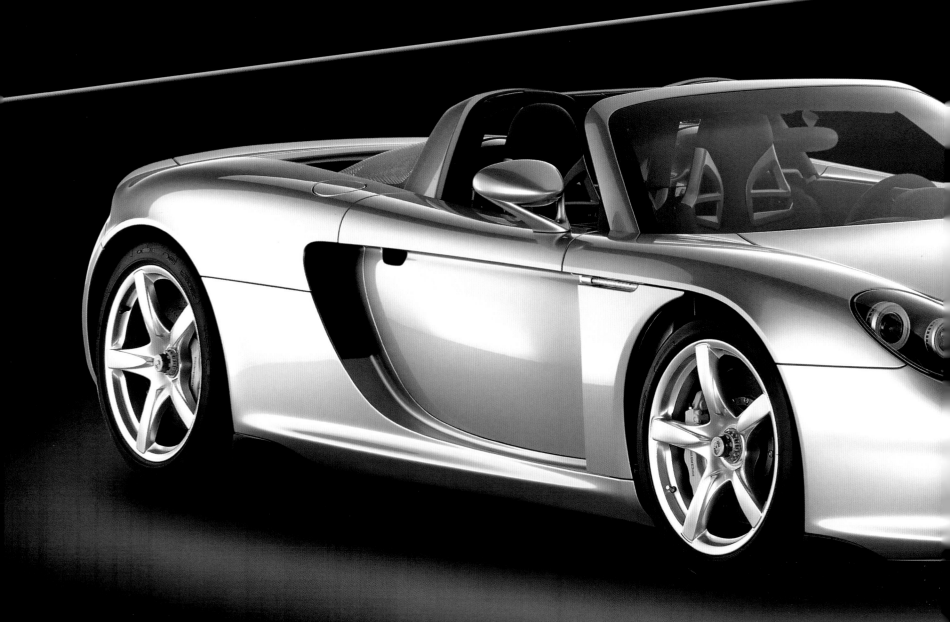

220-221 top The Carrera GT was powered by a 5.7-liter V10 with 612 hp and could reach 208 mph (334 km/h).

220-221 bottom Not only was the Carrera GT one of the fastest vehicles of its day, but it also boasted impressive braking performance – 4.2 seconds to come to a stop from of 124 mph (200 km/h).

This was absolutely extraordinary performance for that time. But the Carrera GT, which weighed 3,042 lbs (1,380 kg), was not just fast it was probably one of the fastest. Thanks to its layout, fine-tuned by former rally champion Walter Röhrl, it delivered exceptional times even on the racetrack and for a few months even held the track record for cars homologated for road use at the Nordschleife of Nürburgring with a time of 7:32.44 minutes.

The Carrera GT was produced at the new Porsche Plant in Leipzig. The initial plan was to build 1,500 units, but in August 2005 Porsche announced that production would end, in response to the increasingly strict US fuel-emission standards, which would have made it practically impossible to market in the US. Officially, 1,270 Carrera GT units were made.

Porsche 911 – 997

In the summer of 2004 Porsche introduced a new generation of car, known in-house as the 997. From a technical standpoint this car, the last one to be designed under the direction of Harm Lagaay. It wasn't that different from the preceding series, but it re-introduced an iconic element that would draw the world's attention - it brought back the oval headlights. It also sported a wider body style, a feature which, for Porsche enthusiasts, made the 997 more enticing than the 993.

At the beginning the 997 was available only in the Carrera and Carrera S versions, both of which had the water-cooled flat six engine. In the 911 Carrera this 3,596 cc engine had a maximum horsepower of 325 at 6,800 rpm and torque of 273 lb.-ft. (370 Nm) at 4,250 rpm. The engine of the 911 Carrera S was bigger by 228 cc, thanks to a 0.12 in. (3 mm) increase in the cylinder bore. As a result it performed slightly better than the base model. Power output at 6,600 rpm was 355 hp, and torque was 295 lb.-ft. (400 Nm) at 4,600 rpm.

Externally, the two models differed only in the tail, which on the S model had four exhaust pipes instead of two, and in the brake calipers that were red on the S and black on the Carrera. However, neither of these distinguishing features could be used to pos-

224 and 225 With the 997, first introduced in 2004, Porsche wisely went back to using the round headlights, a move that was appreciated by its satisfied clientele.

tively identify one model or the other. This was because Porsche Ceramic Composite Brakes (PCCB) with yellow calipers were available as an optional on both models, and because both models came with the original sport exhaust system kit which, regardless of the model, had four exhaust pipes.

In June 2006 Porsche launched a world preview of the 911 Turbo in Germany. This was the world's first gasoline-powered production automobile to sport a turbocharger with variable turbine geometry (VTG). Exhaust gas temperatures (up to 1,832 °F/1,000 °C) were so much higher than they were in the diesel-powered engines, that Porsche had to use special high-temperature resistant alloys. Porsche developed this modern turbocharger in close collaboration with BorgWarner Turbo System. The engine developed a maximum power of 480 hp at 6,000 rpm and 457 lb.-ft. (620 Nm) torque between 1,950 and 5,000 rpm. In the overboost mode the torque could momentarily reach as high as 502 lb.-ft. (680 Nm).

In November 2006 Porsche completed the 997 series with the addition of the 911 Targa 4 and Targa 4S models, both of which, for the first time in the history of the 911 Targa, were exclusively equipped with four-wheel drive. Aesthetically speaking, these vehicles differed from the Carrera 997 in their side profile, which was characterized by the tapered geometry of the rear side windows and in the polished and anodized aluminum trim strips that extended along the edge of the roofline, up from the base of the front pillar, arching along the edge of the roof side support back to the base of the rear side windows. The glass panel roof, made of a specially formulated glass that absorbs nearly all ultraviolet radiation but remains transparent, weighed 4.2 lbs (1.9 kg) less than the roof of the 996 series 911 Targa.

For the 2008 model-year the entire 997 series underwent a redesign. Changes were made to the air intakes and the bumper shields and, for the first time in the history of the 911, the lighting equipment, including the tail lights, turn indicators, brake lights, daytime lights and low-beam lights all used LEDs. Also new as a standard feature were bi-xenon HID (High Intensity Discharge) headlamps. Bi-xenon bulbs were optional for the turn indicators. The all-wheel drive Carrera 4, Carrera 4S, Targa 4, and Targa 4S were had a distinctive red reflective strip between the two rear light clusters.

The most significant difference, however, was in the newly designed Direct Fuel Injection (DFI) engines. These increased power output while also reducing emissions and fuel consumption. Power output of the Carrera and Carrera 4 was upgraded to 345 hp, while for the Carrera S and Carrera 4S it reached 261 kW, or 385 hp.

Porsche's dual clutch PDK (Porsche Doppelkupplungsgetriebe) transmission, made by the ZF Group, was yet another new feature and provided fast, smooth gear changes and an uninterrupted transfer of power. Top speed was reached in sixth gear, while a seventh gear improved fuel economy and reduced emissions. On the S models the suspension was lowered by 0.39 in. (10 mm), thanks to Porsche Active Suspension Management (PASM), the electronic damping control system. This came with two modes - Normal and Sport. For the coupe version that came with the 19-inch wheels, an even newer sporty PASM suspension was available. This suspension was 0.78 in. (20 mm) lower than in the standard version. Its anti-roll bars were stiffer and more downforce was provided at the rear axle.

Starting in model-year 2008 a more powerful version of the 911 Carrera, the Carrera GTS, was also available with 408 hp

226-227 The bodies of both the 911 Coupé and the 911 Cabriolet were developed together. The open-top version had extra strengthening in critical areas. Undoubtedly a beautiful car, especially the Cabriolet.

at 7,300 rpm and 310 lb.-ft. (420 Nm) torque at 4,200 rpm. Engine displacement was 3,800 cc. From the outside, this vehicle differed from the other two Carrera models in its black front spoiler lip, in the modified front apron cooling air intakes, in the different doorsill guards, and in the 1.7 in. (44 mm-) wider body at the rear axle. This model was fitted with 19-inch wheels featuring a central locking wheel nuts similar to those used for racing. The Carrera GTS came as a coupe or as a four-wheel drive cabriolet. All the four-wheel drive versions of the GTS had a distinctive reflective stripe between the taillights.

In 2009 the newly restyled Turbo was unveiled. From this point onwards this model, too was available with direct fuel injection and dual-clutch transmission as optionals. It developed 500 hp. Wheels with the central locking wheel nuts were available by special order.

For the 2009 IAA Porsche introduced a special model, the Sport Classic, a model "focused on the 911 DNA". It took the automaker's Porsche Exclusive department three years to develop it. Only 250 units were produced. At first glance, the most distinctive feature was the duck's tail spoiler whose origins can be traced back to the 1973 Carrera RS 2.7. Its double-dome roof imparted a sportier, more aggressive look to the car. The cockpit was also unusual; it incorporated unique materials, such as a "woven leather," a special material woven out of strips of smooth leather and yarn.

The 3.8-liter engine was tuned to 408 horsepower (up 23 hp) thanks to new resonance intake manifolds. The special model only came with a 6-speed manual gearbox. Ceramic brakes (PCCB), the PASM suspension, limited-slip rear differential, and the 19-inch wheels all came as standard equipment. The Sport Classics were put on the market in September 2009 and all 250 units were sold within the first 48 hours.

In 2010 the new Turbo S also became available. This vehicle developed 530 hp and, thanks to the standard dual clutch transmission, could shoot from 0 to 62 mph (0 to 100 km/h) in 3.3 seconds. The same year, Porsche celebrated the 25th anniversary of Porsche's Exclusive Line by introducing a new special series of the Speedster. Its design paid homage to the 964 series Speedster, and production was limited to 356 units. This vehicle was most recognizable for its shorter windshield and the special double-bubble housing for the soft-top.

A number of elements, such as the classic Fuchs 19-inch alloy wheels, shape of the tail and the exhaust system were also

228-229 The GTS version of the 997 with 408 hp and a maximum speed of over 186 mph (300 km/h). No other 911 model was produced in so many variants. At the end of the day the 997 was offered in 24 different versions.

adopted from the special 911 Sport Classic model. The flat six developed 408 hp at 7,300 rpm; maximum torque was 310 lb.-ft. (420 Nm) at 4,200 rpm.

The vehicle was only sold with a 7-speed automatic transmission, but numerous other features that were optional on the base models came as standard equipment on this vehicle, these included: the Porsche Ceramic Composite Brake (PCCB) package, bi-xenon headlamps, adaptive sport seats, the Sport Chrono Plus kit, the Bose Surround System, leather upholstery, and the leather PCM (Porsche Communication Management) kit.

In contrast to the Boxster, the Cayman introduced in 2005 was immediately met with enthusiasm, if not so much by customers (its sale figures were also inferior to those of its convertible sister), certainly by Porsche enthusiasts and the press. One of the reasons for this is that it was suitably equipped, engine-wise, right from the start, beginning with the Cayman S and its 3.4-liter six-cylinder engine producing 295 hp. A base model that came with the 2.7-liter engine developing 245 hp was introduced in 2006. Another important aspect was that the Cayman is the most enjoyable and dynamic car you'll ever drive, thanks in particular to its stiff chassis.

Of course it goes without saying that the Cayman was the logical follow on of the Boxster's successful sales record and from the standpoint of planning, the most financially profitable one, too. This is further proven by its in-house name. At that time the Boxster was known in-house as the 987 series, and the Cayman as the 987c. The Cayman was first upgraded in 2009, when the engine capacity was increased to 2.9 liters, and the power output to 265 hp, while the Cayman S flaunted a 3.4-liter, 320 hp engine. Thus equipped, the agile coupe almost equaled the 911. But the best was yet to come. At the end of 2010 the Cayman R was introduced with an extra 10 hp and 121 lbs (55 kg) shaved from the weight, not to mention the newly fine-tuned sports chassis. Customers and journalists alike couldn't stop enthusing about the Cayman R. One excerpt from a www.radical-mag.com proof read:

The R should rightfully be lighter, faster and meaner than all the other Caymans. And, in fact, it hits the bull's eye in this regard. And in so doing, it has become a genuine bugbear for the icon of sports cars par excellence, the 911. Not only that, but it's also far more beautiful. The Cayman is the true toy of the Porsche product range, the one that can offer the greatest satisfaction, especially after the recent new edition of the 911. It is more powerful than the Cayman S, inasmuch as the 3.4-liter, six-cylinder engine develops an impressive 330 hp, which is 10 more than the S version.

230-231 No doubt, the Cayman, introduced in 2005, benefited from the fact that the second generation Boxster (the 987), which it was based on, was a vast improvement on the first version (986).

232-233 From day one the Cayman enjoyed a better reputation among Porsche fans and connoisseurs than the Boxster ever had.

Porsche
Cayman

And it's faster, too, even if we are only talking of a few tenths of a second less in its acceleration and a few mph (km/h) more where its maximum speed is concerned. Obviously, it's more expensive, too. On the flip side, with the meaner R version you also get less. Yes you heard right, because most of the 132-lbs (60-kg) weight reduction has come at the expense of equipment. To open the doors from the inside, for example, the complex door handles have been replaced with simple door pulls, vaguely reminiscent of grab handle pull straps for backseat passengers on the Volkswagen Beetle. This modification alone shaves off a good 300 grams…The Cayman R is more than a souped-up S. Its cornering, its precise steering, the ease with which it can fly from one corner to the next, no matter how tight, is truly incredible. Did you take the corner too fast? No worry, just ease off the accelerator and the tail end will turn just enough to take the curve perfectly. If you get taken away with the speed, you can slow down the pace significantly by going into a gentle skid with all four wheels, as long as you have the nerve to do so. After this, you can floor it again and sit back and enjoy the purring cylinders. Obviously, you have to have selected the right gear, because the Porsche's peak power comes on after 4,000 rpm. No sooner have the pumps put the variable camshafts in the optimal position, than the Cayman R becomes a beast to be tamed. One last consideration: the vehicle is by no means uncomfortable, notwithstanding the harder springs and more rigid stabilizing bars. Credit for this, in part, goes to the fabulously sporty seats, but also to the fact that rock hard running gear does not necessarily make the car go faster. Back in Zuffenhausen they'd already learned this lesson a long time ago.

At the end of 2012, six months after the introduction of the third generation Boxster (981), the Cayman was completely renewed as well (981c). As with the Boxster, the wheelbase of the second generation Cayman was also extended by 2.4 in. (6 cm). The base model produced 10 hp more than the previous model, while the S had an upgrade of only 5 hp.

In its first review of the Cayman S, the website www.radical-mag.com wrote: "No, this time we will not question anyone's decision to buy a 911, when the alternative is a Cayman, for the simple reason that the 911 is a 911 and the Cayman is a Cayman. Is it a question of preferring a rear-mounted engine to a mid-mounted engine? Even this is of secondary importance. Is it a question of small and light or big, but still light, then? This would be a comparison of little real value. Is it boxer engine versus boxer engine? A superfluous question. What, then, is the Cayman's mission? What compelling reason is there to buy this two-seater with a hardtop? In other words, why should one even consider buying one? If you know the answer you're lucky… because there is no real reason. After all, the 911 is an icon, while the Cayman is… well, it is just another car in the Porsche lineup. We've had the opportunity to drive the Cayman the way it's supposed to be driven, even to push it to the limit and, in the final analysis, we've found some good reasons to like this small speedster, but we would never trade a 911 for a Cayman, not for any reason.

234 *The Cayman R came perilously close to the 911 - maybe not so much for its looks, but certainly for the sheer driving pleasure it provided.*

235 *Every pound matters. This certainly applies to the Cayman R even though Porsche charged a pretty penny for this slimmed down version.*

Now let's go back to 1996, when Porsche first introduced the open two-seater they called Boxster. This was a small and well-made car but, for some reason, it was never really considered a true Porsche. It seemed to speak more to the aspirations of a beauty salon owner, despite the fact that it possessed qualities that were nothing to laugh at, even when it was pushed hard.

Then, in 2005, the first Cayman came along, designed on the same technical platform as the Boxster. It was clear even then that the two-seater with bucket seats was in a class of its own as far as handling was concerned. The first generation Cayman was a fabulous car, even when compared to the 911 of the day. But times change, and with the next generation of the 911 (the 991 series) the Zuffenhausen team really outdid itself. Maybe it did so just to be able to face up to the Boxster. So, when the Cayman came along, and was based on the Boxster, the result could only be excellent, right? But was it?

Of course, the car drives beautifully, especially the Cayman S, which is equipped with the large, 3.4-liter six-cylinder that delivers a 'mere' 325 hp and yet weighs only 2,921 lbs (1,320 kg) including the highly recommended PDK dual clutch transmission. Not only has the Cayman adopted the Boxster's markedly wider track width, but also everything else that had made us so excited to be behind its wheel, such as the frame's extreme rigidity. According to Porsche you have to apply a force of 29,502 lb.-ft. (40,000 Nm) to twist the car's body by just one degree. Just to put this in context, Bentley's Flying Spur, which weighs 2.68 short tons, or 5,512 lbs (2.5 metric tons, or 2,500 kg), doesn't exceed 24,340 lb.-ft. (33,000 Nm). However, the Cayman is no lighter than the open Boxster, especially because its larger glass surfaces and its large hood offset some of the weight savings. Porsche claims the Boxster and Cayman weigh exactly the same amount, — 60 lbs (30 kg) less than their corresponding earlier models. Credit for this weight reduction comes thanks, in part, to the thin glass used in the rear window and the ample use of aluminum parts. You certainly don't notice this when you are at the wheel. Finally, let's address the ride quality. We tested an S equipped with PDK and the Sport Chrono package. It was a truly memorable experience. The six-cylinder reaches higher revs without the least effort and the new dual-clutch transmission makes shifting gears faster and smoother. All of this you get when the car is in normal mode. The electronic system ensures that the Cayman engages the higher gear ratio even at 2,000 rpm, in the name of maximum efficiency. The Start-Stop function is there as well and works perfectly just as it does on all other Porsches. It's immediately apparent that the absorption ability of the suspension system of the new Cayman is far better than it was in the previous version. The ride, therefore, is far more comfortable. As with the Boxster, you can't complain about the ergonomics either. So what happens when we start pushing some buttons, then? Let's say the road becomes more tortuous and you decide to activate the "Sport plus" mode. The Cayman is instantly transformed. The response to acceleration is at lightning speed, the gears shift only when it is strictly necessary and the running gear becomes noticeably stiffer.

Curves, oh curves, where are you? Ah, here comes the first one. We come into it at full speed: 197 feet (60 meters) before we reach the clipping point we drop anchor (how else would you describe applying the brakes on a Porsche?). The electronics tell the PDK to downshift two gears and now all we have to do is take the curve. The Cayman glides lightly on its front wheels, so we press gently on the accelerator. The tail enters the curve as well and, the moment we've hit the clipping point, we floor it.

238 The Porsche Torque Vectoring Plus (PTV Plus) system is designed to improve traction and is based on variable torque distribution to the rear axle and on an automatic, fully variable rear differential lock. The PTV Plus improves steering precision and feedback by means of selective braking interventions applied to the inside or outside rear wheel on curves.

238-239 The goal of the new Cayman design was to reduce the weight by 104 lbs (47 kg) while at the same time improving resistance to torsion (expressed in Newton meters) by 40%: in the auto world a value of over 40,000 Nm is considered exemplary. The Cayman's is 42,000 Nm.

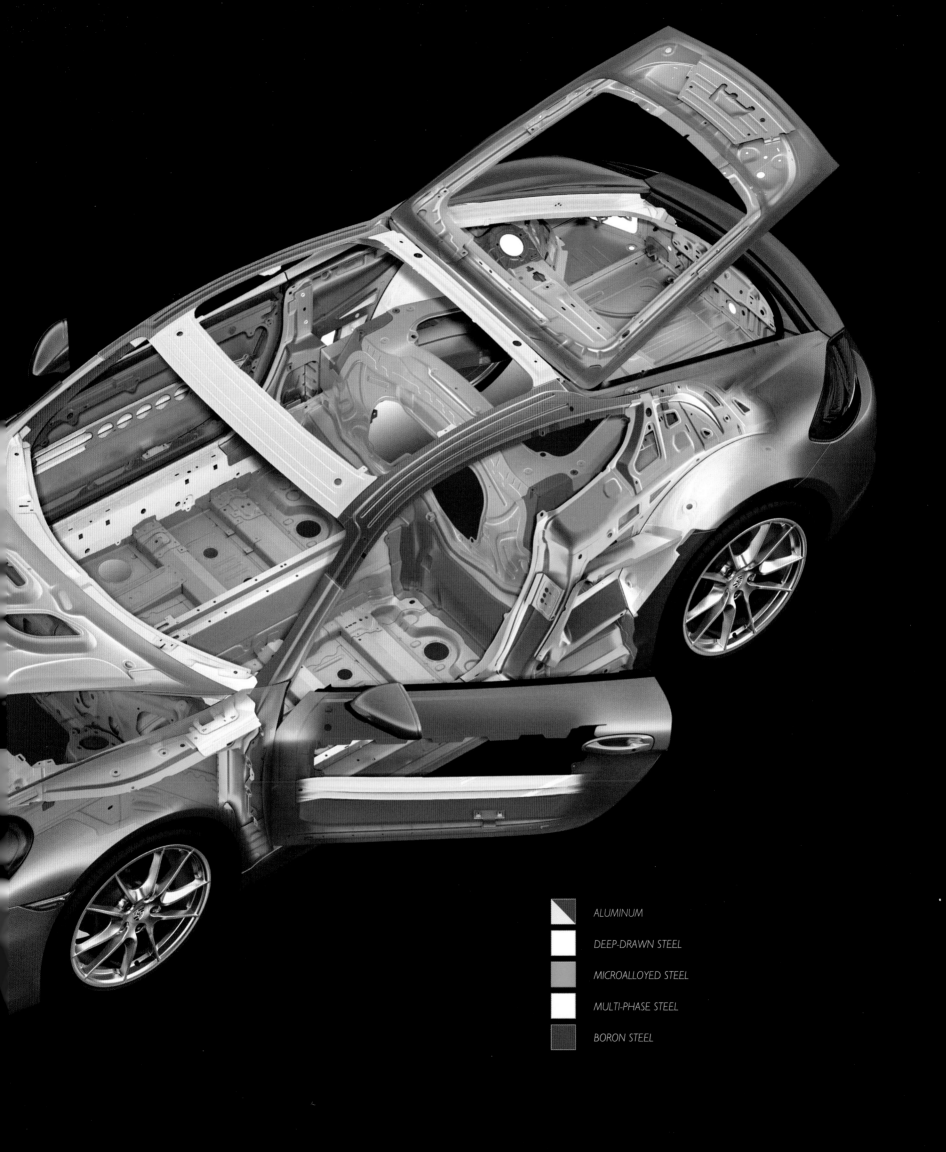

ALUMINUM

DEEP-DRAWN STEEL

MICROALLOYED STEEL

MULTI-PHASE STEEL

BORON STEEL

The twenty-four valve engine discharges the combustion residue from the combustion chambers and screams its way toward 7,300 rpm, at which point it's time to shift gears again. Before you even finish telling yourself to do so, the next gear has already been engaged and the car sprints forward lightning fast. There is no loss of traction during acceleration. The same holds true when you shift up another gear. The only thing interrupting the pleasure of driving is the straight section of road. Not that this means that the S's acceleration potential isn't up to the task, but if it's a drag strip racer you want then there are better cars for the task. Good, now we've left the straight section of road behind us and we can start to have fun again with the next curve. I beg the curve gods, don't let this end! Sooner or later, obviously, the playing around is over and, when the adrenaline rush has finally subsided, we're better able to analyze each of the car's aspects with some objectivity. For example, we can analyze the so-called 'controlled misfire,' or the raucous detonations that are made deliberately by missed fuel injections in the Sport and Sport Plus modes. On a racecourse, while the six-cylinder is growling, hissing and burbling loudly behind the driver's back, this is perfect. But we're afraid the beauty salon owner might drive it like this around the neighborhood, ruining the Cayman's image. For everyday driving, in fact, the Cayman's tone of voice could almost be called obscene. What is the moral? Dear Cayman customers, please don't touch any buttons. The right time for switching your car to Sport or Sport Plus mode will come in due course, but let it be on a racetrack or, at least, outside the city center. We don't know yet whether there will be another Cayman R: Porsche will really have to think about this one carefully, because it might just be a bit too much competition for the 911. The most powerful version (so far) is the GTS. It comes with 340 hp and 7 lb.-ft. (10 Nm) more of torque than the Cayman S: it goes from 0 to 62 mph (0 to 100 km/h) in just 4.6 seconds.

241 It would have been perfectly normal for Porsche to launch a new Cayman R on the market, but the car might have been just a little too much like the 911 for comfort. Enter, stage left, the Cayman GTS.

240-241 The GTS's ride-height is lower, while the engine is more powerful. On the flip side, it offers no shortage of beauty accessories, which make the car more expensive, but don't necessarily make it any faster.

Porsche
Panamera

242-243 The Porsche Panamera won't go down in history as the most beautiful of
Porsches. For the true Porsche enthusiast it's too big, too heavy and, well, not that
elegant. As a car for traveling long distances, grand tourer in the true sense,
it's unbeatable.

There was a time when Porsche would introduce its new models either on its home ground at the Frankfurt IAA or in the neutral territory of Geneva. By contrast, the Panamera was first unveiled worldwide at the Shanghai Auto Show in 2009. This says a lot and clearly indicates that China will probably be Porsche's most important market in the near future along with the USA. The idea that 'bigger is better' rules in China and if truth be told the four-door Porsche probably would have looked slightly less substantial had the market been Europe or even the US. Obviously, this is pure conjecture, but the fact remains that we've seen far more beautiful Porsches than the Panamera with its less-than-elegant rear end. On the other hand, there's no denying that once you're inside or, better-still, behind the wheel, your enthusiasm for the classic Porsche qualities, from driving dynamics to engine power and pure driving pleasure will be rewarded even by this four-door sedan and its large hatchback.

In-house the Panamera is known as the 970 series. Its dimensions are 16.31 ft (4.97 m) long, 6.33 ft (1.93 m) wide, and 4.63 ft (1.41 m) high. It has a 9.51 ft (2.9 m) wheelbase. There's also an extended 10.30 ft (3.14 m) wheelbase version. Officially, the lightest Panamera weighs 3,814 lbs (1,730 kg), but in point of fact the figure is probably closer to 2.2 short tons/2 metric tons.

Initially the Panamera 4/4S was equipped with the same 4.8-liter V8, 400-hp engine that came with the Cayenne, while the Turbo version came with 500 hp. In 2010, however, a basic version was added to the lineup with a 3.6-liter, V6 engine and 300 hp. A year later Porsche made significant additions to the Panamera range. It added the three-liter turbodiesel (250 hp) to the basic range and the Turbo S (550 hp) engine to its top line models. On the technical side, it added the S Hybrid (total output of 380 hp). The 430-hp GTS followed toward the end of the year. Then, at the beginning of 2014, the power of the turbodiesel was upgraded to 300 hp. Other changes have been minor and there was a light restyling in 2013.

244 The Panamera GTS (Grand Touring Sport) was introduced in 2012. With 430 hp, it wasn't the most powerful version, but it was certainly the sportiest..

244-245 Although you wouldn't think that the Panamera was meant for the racetrack you have to admit the GTS version has got what it takes.

The biggest change, of course, is the introduction of the Panamera S E-Hybrid. Porsche already had a hybrid, but this time it decided to go all the way. The new version is a parallel plug-in hybrid: it can be powered by the electric motor alone, by the combustion engine alone, or by the two working in unison. The batteries can be recharged from an electrical outlet. Under optimal conditions, the 9-kW/h power stored in the lithium ion batteries suffices to drive the car a distance of up to 22.4 miles (36 km) on the electric motor alone. For those who aren't just concerned with driving a long distance on the electric motor alone, they can reach a top speed of 84 mph (135 km/h), or negotiate traffic comfortably, without engaging the power of the combustion engine. Used in combination with the combustion engine (a 3.0-liter V6 with volumetric turbocharging), the power output was increased to 416 hp. Thus the sedan would accelerate from 0 to 62 mph (0 to 100 km/h) in 5.5 seconds. A top speed of 168 mph (270 km/h) is certainly not to be sniffed at. If you fully charged the batteries and took it easy on the acceleration pedal, you could get 77 mpg (3.1 liters/100 km).

246 For a hybrid, the Panamera promises well, especially considering the problems involved. The S E-hybrid shows what can be done without sacrificing performance and at the same time maintaining a fuel consumption of only 77 mpg (3.1 liters/100 km) according to certification standards.

246-247 A Porsche station wagon? Why not? The Panamera would be a great starting point.

Porsche and diesel - a touchy subject. For all intents and purposes, this combination had already been tried and proven on Porsche tractors. But in the era of modern vehicles and throughout Porsche history a diesel engine had hardly ever been taken into consideration. Porsche has close links with the Volkswagen Group. The Panamera body is built in Volkswagen's Hannover plant, while final assembly takes place at the Porsche plant in Leipzig. These ties have led Porsche to explore new avenues and the three-liter diesel which the Panamera shares with many Volkswagens and Audis, is among the best of its type. Its main selling point is fuel consumption. The 2.2 short ton (two-metric-ton) vehicle could be driven on an average of just over 1.8 gallons/62 miles (7 liters/100 km), a decidedly strong argument when it comes to a Porsche.

At the end of 2013 Porsche increased the torque of the 570 hp Turbo S by 37 lb.-ft. (50 Nm) to achieve a peak torque of 553 lb.-ft. (750 Nm) in the 2,250 – 5,000 rpm range. With overboost the torque was further increased to 590 lb.-ft. (800 Nm). The Turbo S is also available as an Executive model where an extra 5.9 in. (15 cm) has been added to the wheelbase.

248 The Panamera Sport Turismo is not only equipped with hybrid technology, but also has the latest electronics, including LED headlights and a touch-screen monitor ignition. This, of course, is located to the left of the steering wheel.

249 Just a few years ago the prospect of a Porsche station wagon would have seemed unthinkable. In 2012, however, Porsche unveiled the Sport Turismo at the Paris Salon and it is almost certain that production could begin in 2015.

Porsche 911 – 991

Seen from the outside, the differences between the 911 series 991, marketed since 2011, and the earlier 911 series 997 are not particularly noticeable, even if the wheelbase of the 991 has been extended by a good 3.9 in. (10 cm). At 176.8 in. (4,491 m), the new overall length of the 991 is only 2.2 in. (5.6 cm) longer than the overall length of the 911 series 997.

From the standpoint of the 911 Carrera's stylistic evolution, however, the changes are evident from every angle. Its silhouette, lines, larger wheels and a more convex windshield further accentuate its true sleek coupe character. The most distinctive features of the redesigned and widened front end are the new light clusters and the larger lateral air intakes. At the tail end, the wider retractable spoiler underscores the power increase of the new 911 Carrera models. The new squinting eye design of the LED rear lights completes the car's rear look.

The new 911 Carrera is the world's first standard production car to come with a seven-speed manual gearbox. The transmission is a modified version of the seven-speed dual-clutch gearbox, which is also available as an optional. The close ratio spread of the first six gears guarantees the driver excellent acceleration potential. The seventh gear, practically an overdrive, makes it possible to improve fuel consumption. This is the first time Porsche has equipped a sports car like the Carrera with an engine start-stop system.

Thanks to a completely redesigned body that incorporates significant elements of new design, the 911 Carrera raises the standard in driving dynamics to new levels. The lengthened wheelbase and wider front track generate an innovative geometry with greater tracking and roll stability at high speeds on the straight and on corners. With the introduction of the new electro-mechanical power steering, Porsche engineers have managed to develop a system that, for the first time, combines Porsche's trademark precision and feedback qualities with significant improvements in consumption and comfort.

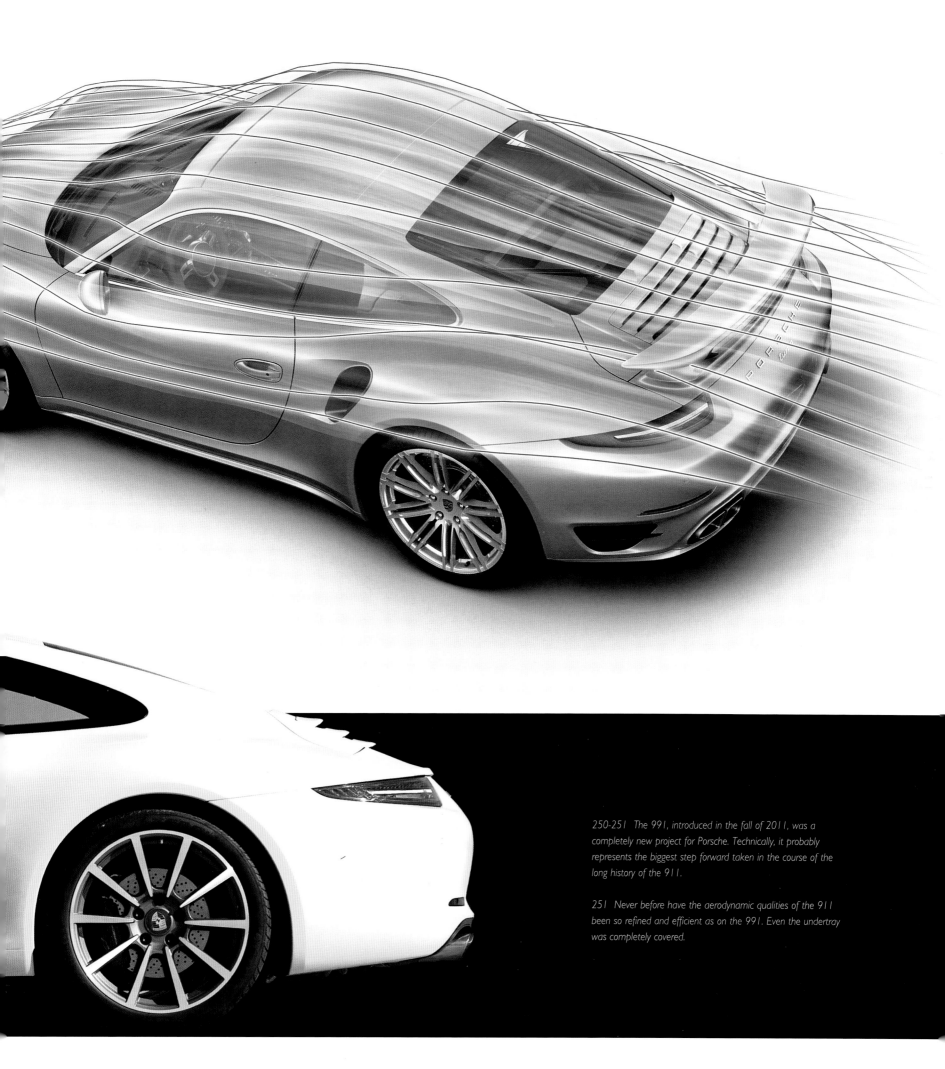

250-251 The 991, introduced in the fall of 2011, was a completely new project for Porsche. Technically, it probably represents the biggest step forward taken in the course of the long history of the 911.

251 Never before have the aerodynamic qualities of the 911 been so refined and efficient as on the 991. Even the undertray was completely covered.

The new active Porsche Dynamic Chassis Control (PDCC) system, available as an optional on the Carrera S, further extends the limits of the vehicle's transverse dynamics. This active roll compensation system detects any vehicle roll on cornering the very instant it begins and then makes practically all the compensation necessary. This was also the first time Porsche used Porsche Torque Vectoring (PTV) on the 911 Carrera S to further improve traction and lateral stability and to reduce reaction to load shifts. This system consists of a mechanical rear differential lock and variable torque distribution to the rear axle in combination with the seven-speed manual gearbox. Vehicles with the dual-clutch gearbox come with the even higher performing PTV Plus, with an automatic, fully variable rear differential lock. Furthermore, the PTV and PTV Plus improve handling and steering precision by means of selective braking interventions applied to the inside rear wheel on curves. The PTV and PTV Plus are also available for the 911 Carrera.

In creating the car's interior, which was patterned after the Carrera GT, the Porsche designers made sure it was in harmony with the new look of the 911 Carrera. The driver is now even further assimilated into the cockpit thanks to the elevated center console with its standard or automatic gear selector, or lever, mounted high and extremely close to the steering wheel in typical racing fashion. The switches for the vehicle's main command and control functions are grouped into logical clusters in the center console. The center of the dashboard, which is completely redesigned, is dominated by the larger, 7-inch touchscreen monitor, via which numerous functions are controlled. The classic Porsche elements, like the five circular instrument panels, with the rev counter in the middle, and the ignition switch to the left of the steering wheel, were obviously carried over to the new model, but the driver and passenger sit on completely redesigned sport seats with four-way automatic adjustment.

In the pursuit of improved efficiency, the earlier engines and transmission systems already offered an excellent starting point. Consequently, for the first time in the history of extending its lineup, Porsche felt that it could afford to take the downsizing route. For the Carrera's flat six, then, it reduced the cylinder stroke by 0.16 in. (4 mm), thereby changing the engine displacement from 3.6 to 3.4 liters. On the other hand, the 3.8-liter six-cylinder of the Carrera S remained unchanged. The Carrera S develops 390 hp, while the Carrera does not exceed 350 hp.

252 and 253 The 40th anniversary of the 911 Turbo also saw the arrival of the latest version, the 991. This version featured all-wheel drive, active rear steering, adaptive aerodynamics and up to 560 hp.

One of the most significant innovations of the 911 Carrera involves its coupe body. The body shell, doors, hoods, fenders and roof, are almost 50% aluminum. Together with its excellent aerodynamics (Cx 0.29), the new combination of aluminum and steel contributes in no small way to the refined goals of Porsche Intelligent Performance philosophy. The idea behind this philosophy is to use the right material for the right part. Liberal use of aluminum to reduce the vehicle's weight, therefore, goes hand in hand with the use, elsewhere, of highly resistant steel that guarantees greater structural rigidity and the maximum protection of the vehicle's occupants. This smart, lightweight-architecture was applied to assembly parts as well through the use of a high proportion of aluminum, magnesium, and plastic parts and the use of optimal upholstery thickness.

Compared to previous models, and thanks to these solutions, about 209 lbs (95 kg) have been shaved off the overall net weight of this vehicle, despite its larger size.

Later, in 2012, Porsche introduced the Cabriolet. Now, while neither the boxer engine, nor the open roof body is a Porsche invention, *per se*, at this point one just has to ask oneself - How on earth do they do it? Every time, without exception, the Zuffenhausen engineers unveil a new 911, the vehicle is an improvement over the previous model. This applies to the cabriolets as well. According to www.radical-mag.com:

"The new open-roof version of the 911 is simply perfect. We have no idea how the Weissach designers managed to achieve such a feat. Harder still to imagine is how on earth they will manage to further improve the newly introduced heir to the 911 five years down the road. It must be truly demoralizing for the German competition in the premium segment to see what Porsche manages to eek out of a car whose roots go back 40 years."

You can read about how to drive this new Porsche in numerous articles about test-driving the Coupe. In theory, there are no substantial differences between driving the Coupe and driving the Cabriolet, even tough the latter is slightly heavier and has a little less pickup than the hardtop version. If you plan to take to the open road to fully take advantage of the dynamic potential of this icon among sports cars, I suggest you first just hand over your driver's license to your police department of choice.

To recap: the 911 Cabriolet is sexy and is therefore more expensive than the Coupe. But what, exactly, are the differences between the open and hardtop versions? Porsche pulled all stops to make sure it would not be easy to tell or feel the difference between the two. The new roof, made of three massive fabric-covered magnesium plates, reproduces the curved silhouette of the Coupe's roof "to a T." If it weren't made of canvas you wouldn't know the difference.

Only the cover to the roof storage compartment, which doubles as the engine hood, gives away the identity of the open-top version. The new hardtop is not only lighter, thanks to its new magnesium components, but it should also be better at absorbing sounds from the outside, because of the additional sound-isolating barrier. Since the introduction of water-cooled engines, no other engine has produced such an engagingly resonant sound as the 991. Unfortunately, the driver can't hear it.

The completely electrically powered roof control system has remained unchanged: it takes 20 seconds to open and close the roof and it remains operable up to a speed of 31 mph (50 km/h). New to this version, on the other hand, is the automatic wind deflector, which can be easily deployed and not only significantly reduces the "hurricane effect" inside the cockpit, but also lets you clip the wings of any windblasts you might encounter. Those who want to use the small rear seats—maybe to carry a golf bag or a *Sachertorte*, just have to lower the wind deflector, pop the goodies behind the front seats, and then raise it again. It's so simple and comfortable you just have to wonder why no one thought of it before.

Soon after it was introduced to the market, the power of the Carrera S was upgraded to 400 hp. Not only are the GT3, GT2 and Turbo versions available, but the Speedster is as well. Starting in 2014 the Targa, aesthetically reminiscent of the original Targa, but with a complex electrically powered retractable roof, will also be available.

254-255 and 256-257 The 911 Turbo (991) is also available in the open version, of course. Never has a Cabriolet been so exciting to drive, or so fast. Want to go over 186 mph (300 km/h)? No problem.

Porsche 918 Spyder

There are two Porsche 918 cars. The 918 Spyder made its world debut at the Geneva Motor Show in 2010 but only went into production in 2013 following a decision of the Porsche Board of Directors on July 28th, 2010. The other 918, the 918 RSR, was based on the 918 Spyder and was first presented as a concept and design study at the Detroit Motor Show in 2011.

When it was eventually produced the 918 RSR differed from the initial concept car. A mid-engine coupe, the 918 RSR is equipped with the 997 Hybrid GT3's innovative technology. The power source of the vehicle consists of the flywheel accumulator, which is able to accumulate its power directly from the vehicle's dynamics when braking. The driver can draw on this power at the push of a button, if necessary, and distribute it over the front wheels by means of two 75 kW electric motors. The number 22, emblazoned on the shell, pays homage to the winning car at the 24 Hours of Le Mans in 1971, the 917 K.

258 The Porsche 918 Spyder exceeded 202 mph (325 km/h) and therefore needed a
new rear spoiler system to add sufficient downforce.

258-259 In full view: the 918 Spyder's top pipes, the upward-venting exhaust pipes
that emerge from the tail, right above the engine. The main advantage of this design is
optimal heat dissipation, because the hot exhaust gases are released via the shortest

But the real thing is the 918 Spyder. This is the car which embodies the essence of Porsche philosophy - to combine thoroughbred motorsport technology with extraordinary everyday drivability, without sacrificing maximum performance or minimum consumption. With the 2013 global debut at the IAA, a new chapter was opened in the future of hybrid drive. This was a flagship project that could quicken the pulse rate of more than just the pioneers of the new technology. The 918 Spyder, in fact, highlights the inherent power of hybrid drive like no other engine has done before. It increases both performance and efficiency without making any compromises between either of these factors. It's the same idea that over the course of 50 years made the Porsche 911 the most successful sportscar in the world. In other words, the 918 Spyder holds the DNA for all future Porsche sportscars.

The 918 Spyder's close links to motorsport are obvious on many different levels. The years of experience in designing Porsche cars for the 24 Hours of Le Mans race have been incorporated into the 918 Spyder. The structural concept of the 918 Spyder with a rolling chassis as its basis — a basic vehicle that can be driven even without a body — is race car tradition at Porsche.

The design of the V8 engine originates from the LMP2 RS Spyder race car. This had a 3.4-liter engine, while the 918 by contrast has a 4.6-liter engine and develops 608 hp. The load-bearing structures, such as the monocoque and the subframe, are made of carbon fiber reinforced polymer. More importantly, the 918 Spyder also far outperforms its competitors in terms of efficiency. Consequently, as a plug-in hybrid vehicle, it combines the dynamic performance of a racing machine with over 880 hp and a consumption of about three liters in the New European Driving Cycle (NEDC) fuel consumption and emission level assessment. This means its fuel consumption is lower than that of most current economy cars. During braking, the energy recovered is stored in a lithium-ion battery located between the fuel tank and the engine and , weighing just under 220 lbs (100 kg). The power is delivered to the wheels through a dual clutch gearbox. The result is maximum driving pleasure with minimum consumption.

The 918 Spyder is built in the historic Porsche plant in Zuffenhausen.

260-261 The 918 Spyder incorporates traditional Porsche good looks with cutting edge sports car technology. Planned from day one as a high performance hybrid, this vehicle reconciles, like no other car, the seemingly contradictory qualities of an 887-hp supercar, with those of a silent, zero-emission electric vehicle.

261 The super sporty 918 Spyder with plug-in hybrid drive ushers in a whole new era in the history of the sports car. Never before has a super sports car suited to everyday use been able to combine extraordinary driving dynamics with the fuel consumption of an economy car.

Porsche Macan

The Macan, the first Porsche in the compact SUV segment, was designed to set new standards for driving dynamics and pure driving pleasure both on- and off-road. The Macan combines the typical handling characteristics that have always been part of the Porsche marque. Top performance in acceleration and braking, outstanding pickup, great maneuverability and surgical steering precision, all served up with superior comfort and everyday practicality.

The Porsche Macan knows how to do everything all other SUVs do, but faster. It's inherently comfortable, knows how to manage the off-road, and can carry five passengers. But, with 400 hp, it simply manages to do all this faster than the competition. So, who will buy it? Probably those who think the Cayenne is too big, and the Cayman is too sporty. Or, maybe, those who already own one of the other two and want to see their wife parking her new car in front of the kid's school. Here the Macan is perfect thanks to its 185 in. (470 cm) length, just that much shorter than the Cayenne so that its tail will not stick out needlessly into the street when the kids are being picked up from school. Sure, obviously you can do the same with an Audi Q5, but this is precisely because the Macan and the Audi Q5 share a not-insignificant part of their platform. The Macan is not an Audi (thank goodness for that you might say) and definitely has a more original line.

The Macan's sports heritage is reflected in its design, just like all the cars that carry the Porsche badge. The Sport Utility Vehicle is well grounded.

The overlapping hood and the gently sloping roofline accentuate the general feeling of sporty elegance and powerful dynamics. The Macan is produced in the Leipzig plant, where Porsche has invested 500 million euro to establish a production line capable of turning out about 50,000 units per year.

In the first stage of its market launch, the Macan product range includes three models. The Macan S is equipped with a 3.0-liter, twin-turbo, V6 engine delivering 340 hp and, like all the Macans, has active all-wheel-drive with an electronically controlled, map-controlled multi-plate clutch. The seven-speed dual-clutch transmission transfers power as required, almost without any interruption in tractive force, enabling the vehicle to accelerate from 0 to 62 mph (0 to 100 km/h) in 5.4 seconds (5.2 seconds with the optional Sport Chrono package). The vehicle reaches a top speed of 158 mph (254 km/h). The front of the Macan S is quite conventional and consists almost entirely of air intakes. On road, the 340 hp of the 3-liter V6 are more than enough to keep the competition in the rearview mirror at a safe distance.

The Macan S Diesel is the more economical version of the Macan trio. Its turbodiesel, 3.0-liter, V6 consumes just over 1.66 gal./62 mi. (6.3 liters/100 km), meeting fuel consumption regulations. At the same time, its 258 hp engine enables it to accelerate from 0 to 62 mph (0 to 100 km) in just 6.3 seconds and to achieve a top speed of 143 mph (230 km/h).

262-263 top The Macan may sport a typical Porsche design, but there's no denying that it's based on the Audi Q5, doubtless to take advantage of the synergies within the Volkswagen Group.

262-263 bottom The design of the Macan clearly borrows features that earned the Cayenne so much success. Nevertheless, the similarity between the two continues to surprise.

The Macan Turbo is the top-of-the-range Macan and is the highest-powered vehicle of the compact SUV segment. Its 3.6-liter, V6 twin-turbo engine unleashes 400 hp, catapulting the vehicle from 0 to 62 mph (0 to 100 km/h) in 4.8 seconds and giving it a top speed of 165 mph (266 km/h). All this power, unfortunately, is not accompanied by a roar. The sound from the tailpipes may be distinctive, but the sportiest of the compact SUVs, as Porsche likes to call it, can hardly be heard. With Porsche, it's always the same - if you want the full sound-effect, you have to be willing to pay for it.

For the Macan, the gasoline engines come with integrated dry-sump lubrication and a modified oil sump shape, which ensures optimal lubrication of the engine (even in extreme driving situations), lowers the vehicle's center of gravity, and increases ground clearance. The diesel engine relies on a pressure-fed lubrication concept with a wet sump. The car maintains a consistent vehicle level, especially with its adjustable suspension. The steering is precise, even if somewhat light, while, as always, the brakes are extraordinary and the lateral body movement always remains in the green zone.

264 As far as dimensions are concerned, the differences between the Cayenne and the Macan are surprisingly few: the small SUV is only 6 in. (16 cm) shorter than the Cayenne.

265 The compact SUV is the most significant player in the new era of automobile design. Naturally, Porsche wants its share of this market; annual production capacity is 50,000 units.

Too bad, then, for those few extra pounds: the Macan S weighs at least 4,112 lbs (1,865 kg), and the Turbo weighs a full 4,244 lbs (1,925 kg). Even those who are experts in weight balance can't perform miracles, because the laws of physics apply to them as well. It would be wrong to say that the Macan gives the impression of a heavy car but, actually, it is. When you eventually get to braking, you suddenly realize that you've got about a two- metric ton load with you. The Macan may be sporty, but it isn't a thoroughbred.

Its name comes from the Indonesian word for tiger and is spot-on. The Macan is powerful and ready to pounce at any time, yet light-footed and tenacious on off-road terrain. The list of optional special equipment offers further treats, such as the air suspension system, which make the Macan stand out from all the competition in the compact SUV segment. Another optional, the Porsche Torque Vectoring Plus system, was specially tailored to the Macan. This system distributes varying levels of drive torque to the rear wheels and works in conjunction with an electronically controlled rear-axle differential lock.

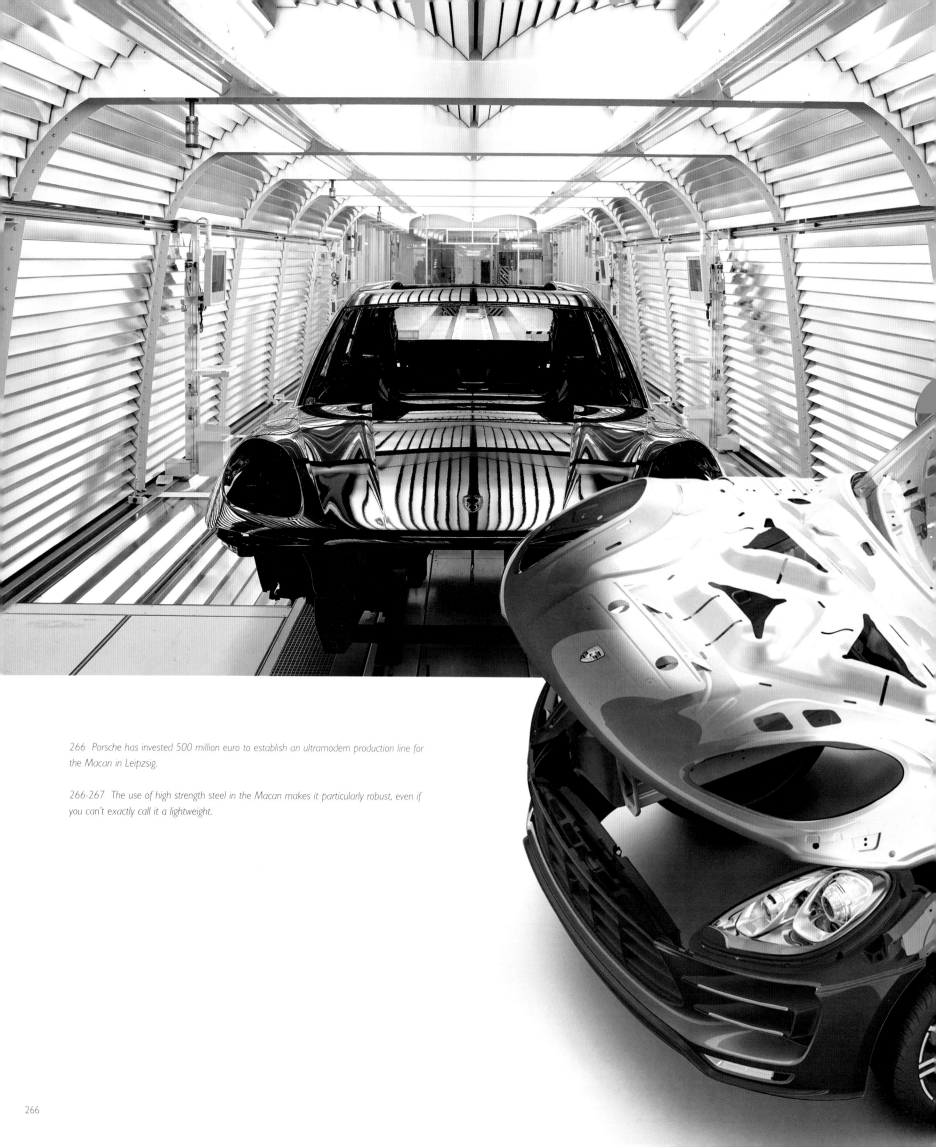

266 Porsche has invested 500 million euro to establish an ultramodern production line for the Macan in Leipzsig.

266-267 The use of high strength steel in the Macan makes it particularly robust, even if you can't exactly call it a lightweight.

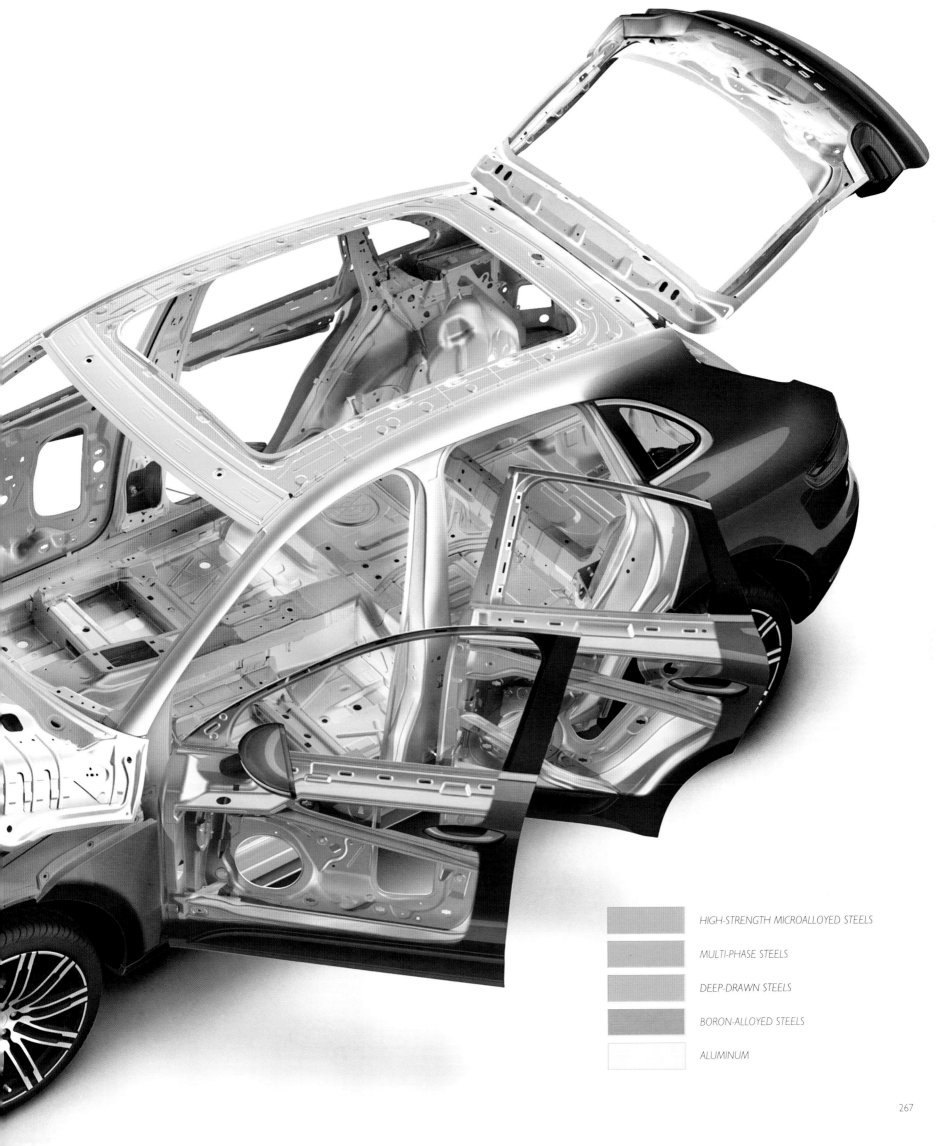

HIGH-STRENGTH MICROALLOYED STEELS

MULTI-PHASE STEELS

DEEP-DRAWN STEELS

BORON-ALLOYED STEELS

ALUMINUM

Author Biography

Peter Ruch formerly editor-in-chief of the well-known Swiss motoring magazine "Automobil Revue" is now a member of the "Car of the Year" international award jury. He is the author of "Panamericana. Mit dem Motorrad von Alaska bis Feuerland" (Diary of a motorcycle journey from Alaska to Tierra del Fuego). His other books include "Cadillac. Standard of the World" and "Mini. Die Geschichte einer Legende" (Mini. The history of a legend). For White Star publishers he has authored "Legendary German cars".

Index

Photographic Credits

Page 3 Ramin Talaie/Corbis

Pages 4-5, 6-7 Ron Kimball/KimballStock

Pages 8-9, 10-11, 12-13 Fotostudio Zumbrunn

Pages 14, 15 Courtesy of the Porsche AG Presse

Pages 18-19 Brian Kimball/KimballStock

Pages 20-21 Fotostudio Zumbrunn

Pages 22-23 Michael Weber/ imageBROKER/Agefotostock

Pages 24-25 Peter Steffen/epa/Corbis

Pages 25 top, 26-27 Nathan Willock/ VIEW/Corbis

Pages 28-29 Nathan Willock/Agefotostock

Pages 30-31 Xu Xiaolin/Corbis

Page 32 Michael Weber/Agefotostock

Page 33 Xu Xiaolin/Corbis

Pages 34-35 Vittorio Sciosa/Atlantide Phototravel/Corbis

Page 36 Friedric/INTERFOTO

Page 37 top, center, bottom Courtesy of the Porsche AG Presse

Pages 38-39 De Agostini Picture Library

Pages 39, 40, 41, 42 Courtesy of the Porsche AG Presse

Page 43 Gerd Pfeiffer/INTERFOTO

Page 44 Courtesy of the Porsche AG Presse

Page 45 top De Agostini Picture Library

Page 45 bottom, 46-47, 48-49 Courtesy of the Porsche AG Presse

Pages 48, 49 Courtesy of the Historisches Archiv Porsche

Pages 50 top and bottom, 51 Courtesy of the Porsche AG Presse

Pages 52 bottom, 52-53, 53 bottom Courtesy of the Historisches Archiv Porsche

Page 54 top Courtesy of the Porsche AG Presse

Page 54 bottom Courtesy of the Historisches Archiv Porsche

Pages 54-55, 56 Courtesy of the Porsche AG Presse

Pages 56-57, 58-59 Ron Kimball/ KimballStock

Pages 60-61, 61 top Universal/ TempSport/Corbis

Pages 62-63, 64-65, 66 Courtesy of the Porsche AG Presse

Pages 66-67, 68-69 Ron Kimball/ KimballStock

Pages 70-71, 72-73, 73 top Courtesy of the Historisches Archiv Porsche

Pages 74-75 Don Heiny/Corbis

Page 75 Courtesy of the Historisches Archiv Porsche

Pages 76-77 Don Heiny/Corbis

Pages 78-79, 80-81 Courtesy of the Historisches Archiv Porsche

Pages 82-83 John Marian/Transtock/ Superstock

Pages 84, 85 top and center, 86 top and center, 86-87 Courtesy of the Porsche AG Presse

Pages 88, 89 top, 90-91, 91 Courtesy of the Historisches Archiv Porsche

Pages 92, 92-93, 93 top Courtesy of the Porsche AG Presse

Pages 94-95, 96, 97 Ron Kimball/ KimballStock

Pages 99, 100-101, 102, 103, 104 Courtesy of the Porsche AG Presse

Pages 105, 106, 107 Courtesy of the Historisches Archiv Porsche

Page 108 Courtesy of the Porsche AG Presse

Pages 108-109, 110-111 Marco De Fabianis Manferto/Consulting D&D

Pages 112-113 www.carphoto.co.uk

Pages 113, 114, 115 Courtesy of the Porsche AG Presse

Pages 116-117 Peter Harholdt/Corbis

Page 118 Courtesy of the Porsche AG Presse

Pages 118-119, 120, 121 www.carphoto. co.uk

Pages 122-123 Fotostudio Zumbrunn

Pages 124-125, 126-127, 128-129 Ron Kimball/KimballStock

Pages 130-131, 131 top, 132 top, 132-133 Courtesy of the Porsche AG Presse

Pages 134-135, 136-137 Fotostudio Zumbrunn

Page 137 Courtesy of the Porsche AG Presse

Pages 138-139, 140, 140-141 Fotostudio Zumbrunn

Pages 142, 143 Courtesy of the Historisches Archiv Porsche

Pages 144, 145 Fotostudio Zumbrunn

Pages 146-147, 148, 149 Fotostudio Zumbrunn

Pages 150-151 Uli Jooss/culture-ima/ Agefotostock

Pages 152, 154-155 Fotostudio Zumbrunn

Pages 156-157, 158-159 Marco Defabianis Manferto/Consulting D&D

Pages 160-161 top, 160-161 bottom, 162-163 Fotostudio Zumbrunn

Pages 164, 165 Courtesy of the Porsche AG Presse

Pages 166-167 Ron Kimball/KimballStock

Pages 168-169, 170-171 Fotostudio Zumbrunn

Pages 172-173 Courtesy of the Historisches Archiv Porsche

Pages 174-175 Ron Kimball/KimballStock

Page 175 top Courtesy of the Historisches Archiv Porsche

Pages 176-177, 178-179, 180-181, 182-183 Ron Kimball/KimballStock

Pages 184-185 Kimball Stock Collection

Pages 186-187, 188 top, 188-189, 190-191 Ron Kimball/KimballStock

Pages 192-193 Courtesy of the Porsche AG Presse

Pages 194-195, 196-197, 198-199 Ron Kimball/KimballStock

Pages 200-201 Fotostudio Zumbrunn

Pages 202-203, 204-205, 206-207 Ron Kimball/KimballStock

Pages 208-209 Brian Kimball/KimballStock

Pages 210-211 Ron Kimball/KimballStock

Page 211 Courtesy of the Porsche AG Presse

Pages 212, 213 bottom Courtesy of the Historisches Archiv Porsche

Page 213 top Courtesy of the Porsche AG Presse

Pages 214, 215, 216-217, 216 bottom, 217 bottom Courtesy of the Porsche AG Presse

Pages 218-219, 220-221, 222-223, 224, 225 Courtesy of the Historisches Archiv Porsche

Pages 226-227, 228-229 Ron Kimball/ KimballStock

Pages 230-231 Courtesy of the Historisches Archiv Porsche

Pages 232-233 izmocars/Izmo/Corbis

Pages 234, 235, 236 top, 236 bottom, 238, 238-239, 240-241, 241 top Courtesy of the Porsche AG Presse

Pages 242-243 izmocars/Izmo/Corbis

Pages 244 top, 244-245, 246, 246-247, 248, 249 Courtesy of the Porsche AG Presse

Pages 250-251 Transtock/Corbis

Pages 251, 252 top, 252-253 Courtesy of the Porsche AG Presse

Pages 254-255, 256-257 Fotostudio Zumbrunn

Pages 258-259, 259, 260-261, 261, 262, 263, 264, 265, 266, 266-267 Courtesy of the Porsche AG Presse

Cover
Porsche Carrera GT, 2003-2006.
© Courtesy of the Dr. Ing. h.c. F. Porsche AG

Back cover
Ferdinand Porsche, one of the greatest car designers of all time.
© Courtesy of the Porsche AG Presse

Acknowledgements

The Publisher would like to thank the Porsche Museum, Stuttgart.

PORSCHE
the story of a German legend

WHITE STAR PUBLISHERS

WS White Star Publishers® is a registered trademark
property of De Agostini Libri S.p.A.

© 2014 De Agostini Libri S.p.A.
Via G. da Verrazano, 15 - 28100 Novara, Italy
www.whitestar.it - www.deagostini.it

Translation: Vali Tamm
Editing: Arancho Doc

ISBN 978-88-544-0838-8
1 2 3 4 5 6   18 17 16 15 14

Printed in China